# CRIMES

## WHERE

## FOOD AND DRINK

## MASKED MURDER

### 40 TRUE-CRIME CASEFILES OF POISONING, BETRAYAL AND DEATH

**JAMES HAMPSTEAD**

# CRIMES WHERE FOOD AND DRINK MASKED MURDER



First edition 2026 | Paperback and eBook

Cover and interior design by Big Fat Web
Published by Upload Makers Publishing | uploadmakers.com

# CONTENTS

# INTRODUCTION

Food and drink are supposed to mean something safe.

They belong to the most ordinary parts of life: the dinner table, the lunch break, the bedside mug, the café meeting, the holiday dessert, the bottle in the fridge, the glass raised in celebration. They are tied to routine, comfort, hospitality, and trust. Most of the time, they pass through our lives so quietly that we hardly notice them.

That is exactly what makes the cases in this book so disturbing.

The stories collected here are not simply about poisoning. They are about access, familiarity, and the corruption of everyday ritual. They are about how something ordinary can be used to lower suspicion, disguise intent, and carry harm in a form no one thinks to question. In these forty casefiles, food and drink are not background details. They are central to the crime itself.

A slice of cheesecake offered in apparent kindness. A reheated curry before a wedding. Tea carried on a tray. A smoothie in a troubled household. A holiday cake passed around the family table. A milkshake, a champagne toast, a bottle left next door, a self-serve salad bar. Again and again, what should have signaled normality instead became the route through which fear entered the room.

That pattern is what gives these cases their particular force.

Many crimes announce themselves through obvious threat. These often do the opposite. They move through trust. A meal shared without hesitation. A drink handed over without alarm. A dessert accepted because there is no reason to refuse it. That is why crimes involving ingestion can feel so invasive. They exploit one of the oldest assumptions in daily life: that what is offered to nourish, comfort, or celebrate is not meant to harm.

This book follows that betrayal across homes, cafés, workplaces, hospital settings, hotel rooms, neighborhoods, and public spaces. Some of the cases are intimate and domestic, shaped by failing marriages, jealousy, inheritance, resentment, revenge, or greed. Others widen into public fear, showing what happens when food or drink becomes a weapon on a larger scale. Some are well known. Others survive mainly in old reporting, legal records, or criminal history. All of them reveal how easily ordinary life can be turned against itself.

They are also not all the same kind of case.

Some involve carefully planned poisonings that unfolded over time. Some turn on a single fatal decision. Some ended in clear convictions. Others remain debated. A few belong to that uneasy category where the legal outcome may be settled, but the wider argument did not end there.

The aim of this book is not to force them into a single template, but to present each case as clearly and cleanly as possible while keeping the focus where it belongs: on the crime, the people involved, the setting, and the reason the story endures.

Because these stories do endure.

Part of that is the delivery method. But just as much of it is the setting. A family table is supposed to feel safe. A cup of tea is supposed to suggest care. A bedside drink is supposed to comfort. A child's bottle or glass is supposed to belong to the background of life, not the foreground of terror. When those assumptions collapse, the crime seems to spread beyond the moment itself. It stains the ritual around it.

That is why so many of these cases feel larger than the object at the center. The poison may be hidden in something small, but the breach is enormous. What has been attacked is not only the victim, but the expectation attached to the act of serving, sharing, or accepting what is on offer.

This book is structured as a sequence of casefiles for that reason. Each chapter begins with a casefile dossier before moving into the story itself: the people at the center, the pressure surrounding the case, the turn that brought the crime into focus, the evidence trail, and the legal aftermath. The goal is not sensationalism. It is to understand how these cases worked, what they reveal, and why they continue to unsettle.

Some cases revolve around notorious names. Others are remembered more through the food, drink, or object involved than through the person who handled it. Some unfold in private homes with almost claustrophobic intimacy. Others spill outward into mass fear, media attention, and public health alarm. What unites them is not simply murder, poisoning, or contamination. It is the deliberate use of the familiar.

A meal should not require suspicion. A drink should not need defending. A dessert should not feel like a threat.

And yet, in the pages ahead, they do.

These cases also reveal something about how danger really works. It does not always announce itself with spectacle. Sometimes it arrives quietly. It sits on a plate. It waits in the refrigerator. It is stirred into a glass. It is accepted because there is no visible reason to question it. In many of the cases that follow, the ordinary object did part of the work. That is what makes the crime feel so cold.

Readers of true crime often remember the most violent scene, the most dramatic courtroom moment, or the most shocking confession. In this book, what may stay with you just as strongly is the plainness of the object at the center. Leftovers. Cocoa. Biscuits. Champagne. Tea service. Protein shakes. Soft drinks. A bottle. A lunch. A cup. These are not exotic objects. They belong to life as most people know it.

That is why the title of this book feels exact. Food and drink did not merely appear near these crimes. They became part of the crime scene that masked murder.

Some of the casefiles ahead are historical. Some are recent enough to feel uncomfortably close to the present. Together they move across decades, countries, households, and motives, but they return to the same unsettling truth: danger does not always arrive loudly. Sometimes it is plated. Sometimes it is poured. Sometimes it is passed across a table with a smile.

The cases that follow are about betrayal in one of its most intimate forms.

Open the first casefile. The table is already set.

# THE CHEESECAKE APPOINTMENT

A slice of cheesecake, a beauty appointment, and a guest who appeared perfectly at ease. This case turns on how quickly everyday hospitality can become the cover for sedation, theft, and attempted murder.

## CHEESECAKE GIFT HID SEDATION PLOT

### CASE DOSSIER

| | |
|---|---|
| Case subject: | Viktoria Nasyrova |
| Location: | Forest Hills, Queens, New York, USA |
| Key dates: | Aug. 28, 2016 \| Feb. 2023 \| Apr. 19, 2023 |
| Victim(s): | Olga Tsvyk (survived) |
| Method: | Sedative-laced cheesecake |
| Legal status: | Convicted |
| Current posture: | Sentenced in 2023; conviction in place |

The visit began in the language of routine. An eyelash appointment in a Queens home did not look like a setting built for violence. It looked small, private, and ordinary, the kind of favor that fits easily into a day.

Viktoria Nasyrova arrived with cheesecake, a gesture that carried its own soft logic. Dessert suggested gratitude. It made the room feel more relaxed before anything had even happened. That detail is what made the case so unsettling.

The poison was not hidden inside a formal family meal or a public celebration. Prosecutors said it was carried into a private beauty appointment as a gift, then folded into a larger plan involving sedation, theft, and impersonation.

The case drew so much attention because prosecutors argued that the motive was not simply robbery. They said Nasyrova targeted Tsvyk because the two women resembled each other closely enough for stolen identity documents to be useful. Both were Russian speakers. Both had dark hair and similar features. In the state's theory, the poisoning was meant to incapacitate Tsvyk and clear a path to use the papers she kept in her home.

That motive gave the case a chilling practical logic. This was not a sudden attack framed as rage. Prosecutors described a plan built on imitation. Tsvyk's documents were not treated as incidental property. They were treated as tools that could help someone else step into her place.

The setting made that theory more disturbing. A beauty appointment depends on close physical trust. A client is invited inside. The visit is small enough to feel informal, and informality lowers suspicion. Food in that setting does not feel like a delivery system. It feels like courtesy. That is why the cheesecake became so central to the case. It fit the occasion better than suspicion did.

The case changed shape once the collapse stopped looking self-contained and the room started looking arranged. Tsvyk survived, which meant investigators had more than a toxic body to work with. She could describe the visit, the dessert, the sudden illness, and the fact that Nasyrova was in the apartment as her condition worsened. When she came home from the hospital, the missing documents and scattered pills gave the scene a different meaning.

At that point, the question was no longer only what had made her sick. It was what story the room was meant to tell. Pills near the body suggested self-harm. Missing identification papers suggested a second purpose. The scene did not look random. It looked staged.

That shift pulled the case toward identity. Once the poisoning, the theft, and the resemblance between the women sat in the same frame, the attack no longer read like a strange one-off assault. It became a compact plan: gain entry through routine, deliver a sedative through a gift, remove the victim's documents, and leave the room speaking a false language.

## Evidence Trail

The evidence prosecutors presented was relatively tight. According to the Queens District Attorney, Nasyrova visited Tsvyk's home on August 28, 2016, bringing cheesecake as a gift. After eating it, Tsvyk became ill, lay down, and lost consciousness. A friend found her the next day and she was taken to hospital. When she returned, her passport, work authorization card, cash, jewelry, and other property were missing.

Lab findings helped anchor the sequence. Prosecutors said residue from the cheesecake container tested positive for phenazepam, a powerful sedative, and that the pills left near Tsvyk's body were also identified as phenazepam. That tied the dessert directly to the staged room. The same substance appeared both in the gift and in the apparent suicide scene investigators said had been arranged around the victim.

The state also said that when Nasyrova was arrested, some of Tsvyk's stolen property was recovered. That strengthened the prosecution's case. It did not rest on one dramatic revelation. It rested on accumulation: the poisoned dessert, the collapse, the staged room, the missing documents, and the recovered property all moving in the same direction.

## Courtroom Snapshot

The trial was heard in Queens Supreme Court. In February 2023, a jury found Nasyrova guilty of attempted murder in the second degree, attempted assault in the first degree, assault in the second degree, unlawful imprisonment in the first degree, and petit larceny.

Prosecutors argued that she had poisoned a woman who looked like her, tried to make the scene appear self-inflicted, and stolen the documents and valuables that could advance the plan. The defense argued that the state's version had not been proved beyond a reasonable doubt.

On April 19, 2023, Queens Supreme Court Justice Kenneth C. Holder sentenced Nasyrova to 21 years in prison, followed by five years of post-release supervision. That result fixes the legal posture clearly. This is a completed conviction case, not an unresolved allegation. Public reporting after sentencing noted that the defense was pursuing appellate options, but the conviction and 21-year sentence remained in place.

**Case Takeaway**
What makes this case so memorable is the way courtesy became method. The violence was hidden inside a thank-you gesture, delivered not across a crowded table but inside a one-on-one service visit. The room was intimate, the object was ordinary, and the ambition prosecutors described was larger than the dessert itself. They said the cheesecake was part of a plan to take more than property. It was part of a plan to step into someone else's identity.

This case widens the ways poison can travel. It does not need a family lunch or a formal dinner. A private appointment can be enough. One visitor, one boxed dessert, and one plan to step into someone else's identity were enough to turn routine hospitality into a crime scene.

---

**But a drugged dessert in New York was only the beginning. Next, a poisoned meal in Britain would turn a wedding countdown into something much darker.**

## CASE 01 CITATIONS

Queens District Attorney, 2023-02-09, Brooklyn woman convicted of attempted murder in cheesecake poisoning of Queens look-alike -- https://queensda.org/brooklyn-woman-convicted-of-attempted-murder-in-cheesecake-poisoning-of-queens-look-alike/

Queens District Attorney, 2023-04-19, Brooklyn woman sentenced to 21 years in prison for attempted murder in cheesecake poisoning of look-alike -- https://queensda.org/brooklyn-woman-sentenced-to-21-years-in-prison-for-attempted-murder-in-cheesecake-poisoning-of-look-alike/

ABC News (US), 2023-04-21, Woman sentenced to 21 years for trying to kill lookalike with poisoned cheesecake -- https://abcnews.go.com/US/woman-sentenced-21-years-kill-lookalike-poisoned-cheesecake/story?id=98725438

ABC News (AU), 2023-04-20, Viktoria Nasyrova jailed for 21 years for cheesecake-poisoning of US doppelganger -- https://www.abc.net.au/news/2023-04-20/viktoria-nasyrova-jailed-for-21-years-for-cheesecake-poisoning/102247092

NPR, 2023-04-21, A woman gets 21 years for trying to kill her doppelganger with poisoned cheesecake -- https://www.npr.org/2023/04/21/1171083112/russian-cheesecake-poisoning-doppelganger-nyc

CNN, 2023-04-22, Viktoria Nasyrova sentenced to 21 years for poisoned cheesecake plot -- https://www.cnn.com/2023/04/22/us/viktoria-nasyrova-poison-cheesecake-sentence-new-york-trnd

## CASE 02

# BEFORE THE WEDDING

In the final days before a wedding, a shared meal became the point where romance, resentment, and opportunity collided, leaving behind a poisoning case hidden inside something utterly familiar.

# LEFTOVER CURRY TURNED DEADLY

## CASE DOSSIER

| | |
|---|---|
| **Case subject:** | Lakhvir Singh |
| **Location:** | West London, England, UK |
| **Key dates:** | Dec. 2008 \| Feb. 10, 2010 \| Feb. 11, 2010 |
| **Victim(s):** | Lakhvinder Cheema (died) |
| | Gurjeet Choongh (survived) |
| **Method:** | Aconite-laced leftover curry |
| **Legal status:** | Convicted |
| **Current posture:** | Life sentence imposed in 2010 with a minimum term of 23 years |

The dinner did not announce itself as important. It was leftover curry in a west London home, eaten while a couple talked about a wedding weeks away.

A fridge. A reheated meal. Valentine's Day plans already taking shape. The room looked ordinary enough to disappear into memory if nothing had gone wrong. Then the numbness started. Lakhvinder Cheema felt his face go strange first. Gurjeet Choongh began to feel it too. The darkness came fast after that. He struggled to stand. She became dizzy. What had looked like a quiet night in became a race to the hospital, and within hours Cheema was dead. Choongh survived, but only after intensive treatment.

What marks this case is the speed. Poison often carries an image of delay, secrecy, and long suspicion. Here the line ran brutally straight from dinner to collapse. Once both people who had shared the curry became violently ill, the meal stopped being background and became the center of the investigation.

At the center was a relationship that had already run out of room. Lakhvir Singh and Cheema had been involved for years. By the time of the poisoning, he was engaged to Choongh and preparing to marry her on Valentine's Day. Prosecutors argued that Singh could not accept the engagement and moved from pleading and pressure into revenge.

That pressure gave the case its shape, because this was not a story about strangers. Singh knew the rhythms of Cheema's life. She knew where he lived, what sat in the fridge, and how ordinary access could pass without alarm. Nothing about the scene required forced entry or theatrical setup. Familiarity did the work.

Choongh's presence sharpened everything. She was not only the surviving victim in the legal record. She was the visible proof that the old relationship had ended and a new one was about to begin. In that sense, the meal carried more than food. It carried the fact of replacement. Trial reporting also referred to an earlier December 2008 poisoning allegation involving Cheema, though Singh was later acquitted of that count.

The illness stopped looking like a medical emergency and started looking like contamination. Both victims had eaten the same curry. Both became gravely ill soon afterward. According to trial reporting, Cheema said as he lay dying that the curry had been poisoned and blamed Singh.

That statement did not decide the case by itself, but it redirected it. Investigators were no longer dealing with an unexplained collapse after dinner. They were working inside a sharply narrowed scene: one home, one meal, one shared source of symptoms, and one relationship already under strain.

There was another shift inside that realization. Prosecutors said the poison was not served in a dramatic moment across the table. They argued that Singh had tampered with curry already sitting in the fridge. That detail stripped the act of ceremony. No toast. No spectacle. Just access, timing, and the quiet expectation that reheated leftovers would not be questioned until it was too late.

## Evidence Trail

The evidence built through overlap. Reporting from the trial said Indian aconite, a highly toxic plant poison, was identified as the cause. Accounts described it as the first aconite poisoning case in England since 1882. Investigators then had to connect that poison not just to the meal, but to the person prosecutors said had motive and opportunity.

Witness testimony was crucial. A lodger reportedly saw Singh take a container of curry from the fridge earlier that day, a detail that helped place her at the practical center of the act. Police also found a plastic bag of brown powder in Singh's coat, which tests identified as Indian aconite matching the poison in the curry.

Choongh's survival gave the case additional shape. She could describe the evening, the meal, and the onset of symptoms from inside the scene itself. The prosecution then built cumulatively across motive, opportunity, witness evidence, toxicology, and physical proof. Each strand invited argument on its own. Together they formed the case the jury accepted.

## Courtroom Snapshot

On February 10, 2010, an Old Bailey jury found Singh guilty of murdering Cheema and guilty of causing grievous bodily harm with intent to Choongh. She was found not guilty of attempted murder in relation to Choongh, and was also acquitted of the allegation that she had previously poisoned Cheema in December 2008.

The prosecution said Singh, driven by jealousy after a long affair ended, deliberately laced the curry with aconite. The defense challenged that interpretation and tried to resist the prosecution's chain of proof. The jury accepted the central murder case.

Singh received a life sentence with a minimum term of 23 years. The conviction and sentence fixed the meaning of the dinner table scene. What first looked like an ordinary meal in a private home was judged to be a deliberate poisoning hidden inside leftovers.

**Case Takeaway**
This case is devastating because it required so little visible disruption. No banquet. No crowded celebration. No elaborate hosting ritual. Just leftovers, a refrigerator, and a couple making plans for a future one of them would not live to see.

It also shows why ingestion cases unsettle people so deeply. The harm moves through something routine enough to lower every guard. Dinner at home should feel like one of the safest scenes in a life. Here it became the route by which an ended relationship turned lethal.

What stays with the case is its plainness. The meal was not memorable until it had to be. The symptoms made it impossible to dismiss. The evidence made it legible. The verdict fixed its meaning.

---

**If one shared meal could conceal so much resentment, the next case shows how poison could move even closer to home, carried not in leftovers, but on a family tea tray.**

---

## CASE 02 CITATIONS

The Guardian, 2010-02-10, "Curry poisoner Lakhvir Singh found guilty of murder" -- https://www.theguardian.com/uk/2010/feb/10/curry-poisoner-guilty-murder

The Guardian, 2010-02-11, "Poison curry killer jailed for 23 years" -- https://www.theguardian.com/uk/2010/feb/11/poison-curry-killer-sentenced

ABC News (AU), 2010-02-12, "Curry poisoner jailed for 23 years" -- https://www.abc.net.au/news/2010-02-12/curry-poisoner-jailed-for-23-years/328468

## CASE 03

# AUNT THALLY'S TEA TRAY

What looked like kindness delivered on a tea tray would come to carry a far darker meaning, as one family's rituals of care gave way to a poisoning story that still feels disturbingly intimate.

## TEA VISITS HID THALLIUM TERROR

### CASE DOSSIER

| | |
|---|---|
| **Case subject:** | Caroline Grills |
| **Location:** | Sydney and Gladesville, NSW, Australia |
| **Key dates:** | May 11, 1953 \| Apr. 1954 \| Sept. 1954 |
| **Victim(s):** | Eveline Lundberg, other relatives also suspected victims |
| **Method:** | Thallium-laced tea and biscuits |
| **Legal status:** | Convicted |
| **Current posture:** | Convicted of attempted murder; death sentence commuted to life imprisonment |

The tea tray belonged to a world that was supposed to feel safe. It came through the front door on a family visit, carrying the soft signals of care.

A cup, a saucer, a plate of biscuits: the kind of home baking that turned a visit into a domestic ritual. In Caroline Grills's case, that ritual became the delivery system.

By the time police focused on her in Sydney in 1953, relatives and investigators had linked a series of illnesses in the family that no longer seemed like simple bad luck. Hair fell out. Sight deteriorated. Speech and strength began to fail. The symptoms were strange enough to frighten people and vague enough to confuse them. That confusion gave poisoning room to work.

What made the case stick in the Australian imagination was the contrast. Grills was remembered as a matronly family figure who turned up with tea, cakes, and biscuits. The gesture was ordinary. The damage was not. Thallium, widely used in rat bait at the time, was colorless, tasteless, and easy to miss until the body had already started to give way.

Caroline Grills lived inside an extended family network where her presence did not look like an intrusion. After the death of her father, she moved into his Gladesville home and remained closely tied to relatives by blood and marriage.

According to the Australian Dictionary of Biography, she was known as "Aunty Carrie," a familiar, thick-set woman in dark glasses who frequently visited with tea and baked goods. That made access easy and suspicion slow.

The pressure in this case is harder to pin to a single dramatic motive than in some others. Police and reporters suspected money, grievance, jealousy, or some private appetite for control, but the surviving record offers no clean answer that explains every suspected victim. That uncertainty is part of what makes the case unsettling. The method looks practical. The motive stays cloudy.

What does appear from the record is the social advantage she had: she did not need to force her way into relatives' homes because she was already a regular, accepted visitor. Tea was expected. Biscuits were welcome. An older female relative helping in the kitchen fit the domestic script of the time so well that it could pass without friction.

Repeated illness stopped looking like bad luck and started to look patterned. In 1953, Sydney was already gripped by wider anxiety about thallium poisoning, and that context changed how the symptoms were read. Strange symptoms no longer existed in isolation. They began to resemble a known danger.

The principal surviving victims in the formal proceedings were Eveline Lundberg and her daughter Christine Downey. Both suffered symptoms consistent with thallium poisoning, and the Australian Dictionary of Biography notes that their condition improved after Grills stopped visiting. That is the kind of detail that changes a family suspicion into an investigative direction. Illness attached itself not just to a house or a meal, but to a person. From there the case widened.

Police did not treat the suspected poisoning as a single household misfortune. They looked backward through earlier deaths in the family, including those of stepmother Christine Mickelson, Mary Anne Mickelson, Angelina Thomas, and John Lundberg, exhuming bodies and comparing the present fear to losses that had once been accepted as natural. A case that might have stayed small became a larger historical pattern with a trail behind it.

That widening changed the meaning of the case. The tea tray was no longer only evidence of one attempted poisoning. It became a key to older deaths and a symbol of how domestic routine had been used to cross the line from care into harm.

**Evidence Trail**
The prosecution case rested on method, symptoms, and the cumulative logic of repeated exposure. ADB records that Grills was arrested on May 11, 1953 and accused in relation to the poisoning of Lundberg and Downey, with thallium identified as the poison. Thallium's notoriety in 1950s Australia helped investigators recognize what had once been easier to misread.

The broader investigation added weight. ADB states that police later charged Grills with four murders and one attempted murder, and that exhumation of two of the alleged victims' bodies revealed traces of thallium. That still carried weight, even though the Crown eventually proceeded only on the original attempted murder charge involving Eveline Lundberg. The case was larger than the count that finally went to verdict.

Contemporary reporting captured the speed of the courtroom outcome. Trove's record of The Sun for October 15, 1953, shows a Central Criminal Court jury finding Grills guilty that day after about 12 minutes of deliberation, and the court imposing a death sentence. The prosecution theory, stripped to basics, was that Grills used thallium in drinks or food offered under the cover of family care. The defense said she was innocent and challenged the way police had assembled the story through relatives and suspicion.

One reason the case still resonates is that the evidence remains rooted in domestic details rather than in any single dramatic revelation. Poison in a family setting. Symptoms that do not make sense until they repeat. Exhumed bodies. A woman whose visits seemed to coincide with decline. The proof was cumulative rather than dramatic, which is often how ingestion cases become legible.

## Courtroom Snapshot

The courtroom result needs careful wording because the public legend of Caroline Grills is broader than the formal conviction. She became notorious as a suspected family poisoner linked to multiple deaths, but the conviction itself was narrower. On October 15, 1953 she was found guilty of the attempted murder of Eveline Lundberg.

That distinction needs to stay clear. The police investigation and the press story reached far beyond a single count, but the legal record should not be stretched beyond what the court actually decided.

As summarized by ADB, although police believed they had a strong circumstantial murder case, the Crown proceeded with the original attempted murder charge.

The sentence was death. Her appeal was dismissed in April 1954. Later that year, the New South Wales government commuted her sentence to life imprisonment, and she spent the remaining years of her life in custody until her death in 1960. That is the stable legal posture of the case: conviction for attempted murder, death sentence imposed, appeal dismissed, sentence commuted by government decision, life imprisonment served until death.

It also explains why the case remained so potent in memory. The courtroom delivered a definite result, but not a complete one. The law fixed one count. Public memory kept circling the larger shadow behind it.

**Case Takeaway**

Grills shows how poisoning can hide inside the oldest grammar of domestic reassurance. Tea offered to a relative. Cakes brought to a visit. Biscuits set beside a cup. Nothing in that scene advertises danger. That is why the betrayal lands so hard.

It also shows why some historic poisoning files stay alive long after the legal record narrows. The formal conviction may cover one act, but the pattern around it can still feel much larger. Here, the law closed around attempted murder while the broader family history remained crowded with suspicion, exhumation, and deaths that never sat cleanly in memory.

What survives most clearly is the method of entry. Grills did not need force, noise, or spectacle. She needed family access and a vehicle that belonged in the hand. The tea tray did the rest.

---

**From a household haunted by suspicion, the story turns next to a very different setting: the workplace, where ordinary lunch breaks became the center of a chilling poisoning mystery.**

## CASE 03 CITATIONS

Australian Dictionary of Biography (ANU), n.d., "Grills, Caroline (1888-1960)," https://adb.anu.edu.au/biography/grills-caroline-10371

Trove / The Sun (Sydney), 1953-10-15, "Smiling Mrs. Grills 'Guilty' -- Death Sentence," https://trove.nla.gov.au/newspaper/page/24818600

Trove / The Morning Bulletin, 1953-08-21, "Woman Committed For Trial," https://trove.nla.gov.au/newspaper/page/5496524

Trove, 1954-04-29, "Mrs. Caroline Grills Fails to Upset Death Sentence," https://trove.nla.gov.au/newspaper/article/99091033

Trove / The Sun (Sydney), 1954-09-23, "Mrs. Grills To Serve Life Sentence," https://trove.nla.gov.au/

Trove, 1953-08-10, "Thallium Found On An Exhumed Body," https://trove.nla.gov.au/newspaper/article/49273773

## CASE 04

# LUNCH BREAK EVIDENCE

The most unsettling part of this case is how long it hid inside routine, where packed lunches, break-room habits, and unexplained sickness slowly formed a pattern no one could ignore forever.

# OFFICE LUNCH EXPOSED CYANIDE KILLER

## CASE DOSSIER

| | |
|---|---|
| **Case subject:** | Klaus O. |
| **Location:** | Schloss Holte-Stukenbrock, Germany |
| **Key dates:** | 2018 \| 2019 |
| **Victim(s):** | One co-worker later died after severe kidney damage \| multiple others injured |
| **Method:** | Workplace toxic lunch contamination |
| **Legal status:** | Convicted |
| **Current posture:** | Sentenced in 2019 to life imprisonment |

The sandwiches were the least remarkable objects in the building. They were lunches brought from home, set down in a shared workplace, the kind of meal that belongs to break rooms, lockers, and the repeated rhythm of shifts.

In Germany in 2018, investigators began to suspect that those ordinary packed lunches were not simply food left unattended between tasks. They were the route. Once that possibility hardened, the case changed from workplace unease into something much colder: a poisoning prosecution built not on one dramatic serving, but on the quiet vulnerability of co-workers who expected their lunch to be safe.

Klaus O. worked in a factory in Schloss Holte-Stukenbrock. The case against him did not begin with a family dispute, a holiday meal, or a domestic ritual. That difference matters. The pressure here came from repetition and proximity. Prosecutors said he had been poisoning fellow employees over time by contaminating their food in a place where trust was practical rather than emotional. People left sandwiches and other packed meals in a shared environment because that is what workers do. The state's case turned that habit into vulnerability.

Suspicion hardened when concerns at the factory stopped looking like coincidence. ABC reported that hidden-camera footage captured Klaus O. tampering with a co-worker's sandwich. That moment gave the investigation its center. It was no longer a vague fear that somebody in the workplace might be causing harm. Investigators now had a direct visual link between the accused and a served lunch. From there, the case widened backward. Authorities began examining earlier illnesses and deaths among co-workers, asking whether what had looked like isolated medical tragedies formed part of the same pattern.

## Evidence Trail

Reporting said investigators found toxic substances, including mercury, lead, and cadmium, associated with the tampering. The prosecution linked Klaus O. to a series of poisonings that left multiple co-workers with severe kidney damage and were suspected in one colleague's death, although the court stopped short of treating that death as proven murder.

The hidden-camera footage mattered because it fixed the act in a concrete workplace setting. This was not only a toxicology case. It was also a surveillance case. The visual evidence, combined with the medical harm suffered by the victims, gave prosecutors a route, a pattern, and a defendant tied to both.

## Courtroom Snapshot

In 2019, a court in Bielefeld sentenced Klaus O. to life in prison, with preventive detention, for multiple counts of attempted murder and serious bodily harm arising from poisoning his colleagues' food at work, according to ABC and The Guardian. The prosecution case was that he had deliberately poisoned colleagues' sandwiches and other food items at work over a period of years.

The defense did not prevent conviction. The sentence and preventive-detention order fix the case as a completed conviction, not an unresolved suspicion. The court accepted that the ordinary setting of a lunch break had been turned into a delivery system for long-term harm.

## Case Takeaway

This case stands apart from many others because the meal is neither intimate nor ceremonial. No one is invited in. No family table is set. The lunch is simply there, waiting to be eaten between shifts. That is what gives the case its particular chill. Workplace routine can feel impersonal, but it still runs on trust.

People assume that what they bring for lunch will remain theirs, unchanged, and safe. This case broke that assumption. A sandwich became evidence, and an ordinary break became the point where the workday and the criminal case met.

---

**And if a packed lunch could become a weapon, so could something blended and poured at home, where family fracture and violence would gather around two seemingly harmless drinks.**


## CASE 04 CITATIONS

ABC News (AU), 2019-03-08, German man gets life for poisoning co-workers' sandwiches -- https://www.abc.net.au/news/2019-03-08/german-man-gets-life-for-poisoning-co-workers-sandwiches/10881760

The Guardian, 2019-03-07, German who poisoned co-workers' sandwiches receives life sentence -- https://www.theguardian.com/world/2019/mar/07/german-who-poisoned-co-workers-sandwiches-receives-life-sentence

## CASE 05

# THE SMOOTHIE AND THE GLASS

At the heart of this case is not just poisoning, but family fracture, control, and violence, all centered on two drinks that seemed harmless until the evidence gave them a far darker meaning. What followed would turn an ordinary domestic setting into the scene of a deeply disturbing crime.

## SMOOTHIE AND JUICE SEALED FATE

### CASE DOSSIER

| | |
|---|---|
| **Case subject:** | Sofia Sam and Arun Kamalasanan |
| **Location:** | Epping, Melbourne, Victoria, Australia |
| **Key dates:** | Oct. 13-14, 2015 \| 2018 \| June 21, 2018 |
| **Victim(s):** | Sam Abraham |
| **Method:** | Sleeping pills in a smoothie, followed by cyanide-laced orange juice |
| **Legal status:** | Convicted |
| **Current posture:** | Both convicted of murder and sentenced in 2018; one sentence later reduced on appeal |

A glass can look too ordinary to hold suspicion. In this case, that ordinariness did part of the work. Sam Abraham was at home in Epping, with his wife and small child nearby, when the sequence that ended his life was set in motion.

By the time he collapsed, prosecutors said the fatal acts had already been broken into stages: first a smoothie used to sedate him, then a second drink administered while he was vulnerable. What made the case land with such force was not spectacle but control. The prosecution case, later accepted by the jury, was built around liquids served inside a familiar home and around the claim that an affair had hardened into a coordinated plan to kill.

Sam Abraham lived with his wife, Sofia Sam, and their young son in Melbourne's northern suburbs. Reporting on the trial described a household that, from the outside, still carried the appearance of ordinary domestic life. Inside it, prosecutors said, another loyalty had already taken hold. Sofia Sam had entered a relationship with Arun Kamalasanan, and the Crown argued that the affair became the pressure point around which the case turned.

This was not a public confrontation or a sudden act of visible rage. It was, according to the prosecution, a concealed domestic conspiracy shaped by intimacy, secrecy, and the desire to remove the husband who stood in the way of the future the pair wanted. Coverage in both Australia and India also noted that all three were from Kerala, a detail that helped explain the case's reach beyond Melbourne once charges were laid.

Investigators eventually focused on the drinks themselves. The prosecution case was that Arun Kamalasanan first gave Sam Abraham an avocado smoothie containing sleeping tablets, then later forced cyanide-laced orange juice down his throat while he slept.

That sequence changed the meaning of the death. What might initially have looked like an unexplained collapse became, in the Crown's reconstruction, a staged poisoning carried out in steps. Reporting on the case also pointed to an earlier alleged attempt on Sam Abraham's life at a railway station months before the fatal attack, a detail prosecutors used to argue that the killing had not emerged from a single impulsive night but had grown out of an existing plan.

Once the investigation settled on that structure, the central questions were no longer medical alone. They became questions of preparation, cooperation, and whether the wife and her lover had acted together.

## Evidence Trail

The case was proved through accumulation rather than theatrical revelation. Reporting on the trial emphasized toxicology, the affair between Sofia Sam and Arun Kamalasanan, and the prosecution's reconstruction of the sequence inside the house. The Crown said the first drink created vulnerability, made Sam Abraham easier to control, and the second turned that vulnerability fatal. That two-stage pattern gave the case its distinctive shape. It was not just an allegation of poison in a glass, but an allegation of one served liquid preparing the ground for another.

Prosecutors also relied on the wider relationship evidence and on the jury's acceptance that the death was homicide, not accident or natural illness. By verdict, the home sequence had become the spine of the case: sedation, vulnerability, cyanide, collapse.

## Courtroom Snapshot

Sofia Sam and Arun Kamalasanan were tried in the Supreme Court of Victoria and, in early 2018, a jury found them guilty of murdering Sam Abraham with cyanide. On June 21, 2018, Justice Paul Coghlan sentenced Arun to 27 years in prison with a non-parole period of 23 years, and Sofia to 22 years with a non-parole period of 18 years. The prosecution case was that the pair had worked together to poison Sam Abraham so they could continue their relationship without him.

The defense did not dislodge the toxicology evidence or the broader planning case accepted by the jury. Later reporting said Arun's total sentence was reduced on appeal to 24 years with parole eligibility after 20 years. That legal outcome is what fixed the prosecution theory in court: this was a deliberate cyanide murder carried out through familiar domestic acts, with sleep itself used as part of the method.

## Case Takeaway

The force of this case does not come from a crowded table or a ceremonial meal. It comes from the quiet precision of the sequence prosecutors described and the jury accepted: sedation first, cyanide second, then collapse. The domestic setting did not weaken the case. It sharpened it.

A smoothie, a glass of orange juice, and a sleeping victim were enough to turn an affair into a murder prosecution and, ultimately, into convictions.

---

**The next case takes that betrayal into an earlier era, where a sweet treat passed in public carried a danger no one could see until it was far too late.**

## CASE 05 CITATIONS

SBS Malayalam, Wife and ex-lover jailed for murdering husband with cyanide -- https://www.sbs.com.au/language/malayalam/en/article/wife-and-ex-lover-jailed-for-murdering-husband-with-cyanide/96xsazso5

SBS Punjabi, Sofia Sam and lover Arun Kamalasanan found guilty of husband's murder -- https://www.sbs.com.au/language/punjabi/en/article/sofia-sam-and-lover-arun-kamalasanan-found-guilty-of-husbands-murder/7aulx3twu

Onmanorama, Sam Abraham murder in Melbourne: Keralite wife, lover get jail -- https://www.onmanorama.com/news/kerala/2018/06/21/sam-abraham-murder-case-wife-sofia-jail-term.html

The News Minute, Kerala man's murder in Melbourne: sentence of wife's lover reduced by 3 years -- https://www.thenewsminute.com/news/kerala-mans-murder-melbourne-sentence-wife-s-lover-reduced-3-years-107355

Victorian Supreme Court, live audiocast notice for DPP v Sofia Sam and DPP v Arun Kamalasanan -- https://www.supremecourt.vic.gov.au/news/live-audiocast-of-dpp-v-sofia-sam-and-dpp-v-arun-kamalasanan

## CASE 06

# CHOCOLATE CREAM KILLER

The horror of this case lies in its simplicity: a sweet treat, no visible cause for alarm, and a method that turned casual trust into sudden and public danger.

## BOX OF CHOCOLATES CARRIED DEATH

### CASE DOSSIER

| | |
|---|---|
| **Case subject:** | Christiana Edmunds |
| **Location:** | Brighton, Sussex, England, UK |
| **Key dates:** | 1870-1871 \| Jan. 1872 |
| **Victim(s):** | Sidney Albert Barker (and extra victims) |
| **Method:** | Strychnine-laced chocolate creams |
| **Legal status:** | Convicted |
| **Current posture:** | Murder conviction entered in 1872; death sentence respited and commuted on grounds of insanity |

At Maynard's in Brighton, chocolate creams sat where sweets were supposed to sit: boxed, labeled, and ready to be bought without hesitation.

That ordinary setting is what gave the Christiana Edmunds case its reach. These were not chocolates passed across one private table and then gone. Historical accounts say poisoned creams moved through parcels, purchases, and returns to the shop itself, turning the confectioner's counter into part of the danger. Once that happened, the case stopped being only about one household. It became a public scare, with trial reporting and later historical work describing how the poisoned chocolates reached the Beard household, sickened Maynard's customers, and ultimately killed four-year-old Sidney Albert Barker.

Historical accounts say Edmunds became infatuated with the married Dr. Charles Beard and that their relationship lasted about a year before he ended it in the summer of 1870. That private obsession matters because it helps explain how the danger first gathered around one household. Emily Beard survived after eating poisoned chocolate creams, but her illness became one of the central anchors of the later prosecution. Historians and summaries suggest what began as a targeted attempt against the Beard family widened into something far less containable.

Edmunds was described as repeatedly buying chocolates, sometimes sending children to purchase them for her, and then returning boxes to Maynard's in a way that, once the poisonings were connected, drew investigators back toward her. The pressure in the case comes from that widening circle. A personal fixation did not stay private. It moved outward through an ordinary shop and exposed strangers who had no reason to think a box of sweets could carry deliberate harm.

The poisonings stopped looking like isolated misfortune once the illnesses began to form a pattern around the chocolates themselves. The prosecution theory was that Edmunds bought chocolate creams from Maynard's, adulterated them with strychnine, and then either returned them to the shop or sent them out anonymously, allowing the danger to travel without her standing beside it. Sidney Albert Barker's death gave the case its irreversible center.

The four-year-old died after eating chocolates bought from Maynard's while visiting Brighton in June 1871. At the time, the inquest did not settle the matter in the clean, finished way later retellings sometimes imply. But once the broader poisonings were linked, Barker's death became the confirmed fatal outcome of a campaign that had already made other people violently ill.

## Evidence Trail

The evidence trail was diffuse in one sense and sharply focused in another. There was no single family dinner, one bottle, or one room in which the act could be fixed and finished. Instead there were repeated purchases, poisoned sweets, surviving victims, and one dead child. The attempted murder charge involving Emily Beard and the murder charge involving Sidney Albert Barker gave the authorities two clear legal anchors.

Later historical accounts describe Edmunds paying children to buy chocolates, tampering with them, and putting them back into circulation. That detail is what keeps the case so unsettling. The danger did not remain inside a private relationship.

It moved through a public sweetshop and into ordinary buying habits. A confectioner's counter, a returned box, a visiting child, and a poison hidden inside something purchased for pleasure became the structure of the proof.

**Courtroom Snapshot**

Edmunds was eventually charged with the attempted murder of Emily Beard and the murder of Sidney Albert Barker. Her trial began in Brighton but was moved to the Central Criminal Court, where in January 1872 she was convicted of Barker's murder. Contemporary reporting described the jury returning a guilty verdict after a short deliberation. She was sentenced to death. After sentencing, she claimed to be pregnant, but examination did not bear that out.

Later commentary notes that the sentence was respited and then commuted on grounds of insanity, and she was confined in Broadmoor for the rest of her life. Historians still debate the extent of her actual mental illness, but the legal shape of the case is clear: a murder conviction, a death sentence, and an executive decision that redirected the case away from execution and into permanent institutional confinement.

**Case Takeaway**

What gives the Edmunds case its lasting force is the way poison left the household without losing the intimacy of ordinary consumption. Chocolates are bought casually, given lightly, and eaten without ritual. That is what made the Brighton poisonings so destabilizing.

People did not need to know Christiana Edmunds personally to be put at risk by what she set in motion. Even so, the case never stops being personal. The Beard household remains the starting point, even as the danger moves outward through the town. A private fixation widened into public exposure, and one confirmed child death fixed the horror in the historical record.

---

**From poisoned chocolates in Victorian Britain, the story moves to an icy American lake, where one quiet morning drink would become part of a far more intimate and modern suspicion.**

## CASE 06 CITATIONS

Brighton & Hove Museums, Death by Chocolate? -- https://brightonmuseums.org.uk/discovery/history-stories/death-by-chocolate/

North Laine History, Christiana Edmunds -- http://www.northlainehistory.me.uk/christiana-edmunds.html

The Spectator, Christina Edmunds, the Brighton chocolate-poisoner -- https://archive.spectator.co.uk/article/20th-january-1872/1/christina-edmunds-the-brighton-chocolate-poisoner-

Women's History Network, The Case of the Chocolate Cream Killer -- https://womenshistorynetwork.org/the-case-of-the-chocolate-cream-killer-the-poisonous-passion-of-christiana-edmunds/

Wikipedia, Christiana Edmunds -- https://en.wikipedia.org/wiki/Christiana_Edmunds

JAMES HAMPSTEAD

46

# THE DRINK BEFORE DAWN

**Before the day had even begun, one drink set off a chain of events that would pull money troubles, toxicology, and a death on the water into the same grim frame.**

## SUNRISE BOAT TRIP ENDED IN POISON

### CASE DOSSIER

| | |
|---|---|
| **Case subject:** | Lori Isenberg |
| **Location:** | Lake Coeur d'Alene, Idaho, USA |
| **Key dates:** | Feb. 13, 2018 \| Feb. 2021 \| May 2021 |
| **Victim(s):** | Larry Isenberg |
| **Method:** | Toxic substance administered |
| **Legal status:** | Convicted |
| **Current posture:** | Resolved by Alford plea to second-degree murder; life sentence |

It was still cold enough to make the lake feel empty. Before sunrise on February 13, 2018, Lori and Larry Isenberg took a small boat onto Lake Coeur d'Alene.

Later, Lori told investigators that her husband had gone overboard after the motor stalled, that she had tried to reach him, and that the morning had turned disastrous in seconds. For a while, that account gave the scene its shape. A missing man. Dark water. A delayed emergency call. But when Larry Isenberg's body was recovered and toxicology results came back, the center of the case shifted. The decisive act was no longer the fall into the water. It was what had entered his system before he went under.

Larry Isenberg was 68, a longtime local public-works employee and respected community figure in Coeur d'Alene. Lori Isenberg was a nonprofit executive who, around the time of Larry's death, was coming under scrutiny over missing funds at the housing coalition she led. That gave the murder case a broader frame. Investigators and reporters increasingly saw the lake death alongside the financial collapse closing in around her. The pressure was not just marital. It was legal, financial, and reputational. A sunrise boat ride could be seen as a private outing between spouses, but after the toxicology findings investigators and prosecutors read it as a carefully chosen setting.

The lake search did not change the case. The toxicology result did. Searchers found Larry Isenberg's remains about a month after he disappeared. An autopsy concluded he had a lethal level of diphenhydramine, the active ingredient in Benadryl, in his system and ruled his death a homicide from diphenhydramine toxicity rather than an accidental drowning.

That finding moved the case onto new ground at once. Prosecutors later argued that Lori Isenberg poisoned him and then used the lake to stage the rest.

Her public explanations did not help her. She wrote an email to friends describing the morning in detail. She told detectives she waited before calling for help because she did not want to leave the area where he fell. As the record grew, those details stopped sounding like grief and started sounding like structure.

**Evidence Trail**
The evidence was a blend of toxicology, timing, and surrounding motive. Toxicology was the anchor. The delayed 911 call also sharpened the prosecution case. Court records and reporting emphasized the drug level in Larry Isenberg's system and Lori Isenberg's delay in seeking help. Prosecutors argued that the overall pattern of her actions looked less like panic on the water than a staged accident.

At the same time, the federal fraud case gave the state murder case a sharp financial backdrop. In 2019, Lori Isenberg pleaded guilty in federal court to wire fraud and theft from a federal program, admitting she stole more than $570,000 from the housing coalition she led. She later received a five-year federal sentence in that case. The murder prosecution did not need the fraud case to prove Larry's death, but it gave the court a clearer picture of the financial and legal pressure closing in around her life. By the time the homicide case approached trial, the lake outing no longer stood alone as a puzzling morning accident. It sat inside a broader pattern of concealment and collapse.

## Courtroom Snapshot

In 2020, Lori Isenberg was charged with first-degree murder in Kootenai County. In mid-February 2021, she entered an Alford plea to second-degree murder, acknowledging that the prosecution had sufficient evidence to convict while not admitting guilt outright.

The prosecution theory was that she fatally poisoned Larry Isenberg with diphenhydramine before or during the pre-dawn outing and then presented the death as a fall overboard. Public reporting also preserved one of Lori Isenberg's later claims: that the drugged drink had been intended for herself, not for Larry. The court was not required to accept that explanation.

In late May 2021, she was sentenced to life in prison with a minimum of 30 years before parole eligibility. The Alford plea and sentence mean Larry Isenberg's death is formally recorded as a homicide, not an accident, and the original boating-accident account no longer stands in the legal record.

## Case Takeaway

This case is hard to separate from its setting. A lake at dawn can make almost any story sound plausible for a few hours. Motors fail. People slip. Cold water swallows evidence fast. But this case held because the water was never the whole story. Toxicology, delay, and financial pressure kept pulling it back to shore.

The poison did not move through a family dinner table or a holiday ritual. It moved through a drink on an outing that should have looked private, ordinary, and harmless. In the end, this became a case about staging as much as poisoning. The calm surface did part of the work. The record undid it.

---

**But the use of poison did not belong only to domestic relationships. In the next case, it entered the routines of working life, carried in the simplest object of all: a cup of tea.**

## CASE 07 CITATIONS

The Spokesman-Review, Lori Isenberg pleads guilty to killing her husband on Lake Coeur d'Alene in 2018 -- https://www.spokesman.com/stories/2021/feb/11/lori-isenberg-pleads-guilty-to-killing-husband-on-/

The Spokesman-Review, Lori Isenberg sentenced to life for killing husband by drugging him on boat on Lake Coeur d'Alene -- https://www.spokesman.com/stories/2021/may/24/isenberg-sentenced-to-life-for-drugging-husband-on/

U.S. Department of Justice, Lori Isenberg Sentenced in Wire Fraud and Federal Program Theft Case Involving Over $570,000 -- https://www.justice.gov/usao-id/pr/lori-isenberg-sentenced-wire-fraud-and-federal-program-theft-case-involving-over-570000

People, An Idaho Grandma Poisoned Her Husband During a Sunrise Boat Ride. Here's Where Lori Isenberg Is Now -- https://people.com/where-is-lori-isenberg-now-after-poisoning-husband-11910240

52

## CASE 08

# THE TEACUP POISONER

Some killers hide in chaos. This one hid in repetition, using the ordinary habits of working life to mask a pattern of poisoning that feels cold, methodical, and strangely detached.

## TEACUPS TURNED TOXIC AT HOME

### CASE DOSSIER

| | |
|---|---|
| **Case subject:** | Graham Young |
| **Location:** | Bovingdon, Hertfordshire, England, UK |
| **Key dates:** | 1971 \| 1972 |
| **Victim(s):** | Fred Biggs \| multiple co-workers sickened |
| **Method:** | Thallium-laced tea and workplace drinks |
| **Legal status:** | Convicted |
| **Current posture:** | Sentenced to life imprisonment in 1972; died in custody in 1990 |

A cup of tea is supposed to disappear into the workday. It is poured, sweetened, lifted, and forgotten. That is what made the Graham Young case so unnerving.

At a factory in Bovingdon, the familiar rhythm of tea breaks became the setting for repeated thallium poisonings built not on spectacle but on repetition. People felt unwell, recovered, then fell ill again. The pattern did not announce itself as violence at first. It looked like ordinary sickness moving through an ordinary workplace. When Fred Biggs died, the same small object that should have marked a pause in the day began to look like evidence. The case that followed fixed one of Britain's most enduring poisoning nicknames to a man whose method depended on how completely a drink could vanish into routine.

Young had previously poisoned members of his own family as a teenager, including his stepmother, and had been detained in Broadmoor before later being released. That history matters because the workplace poisonings did not come from nowhere.

But the force of this case does not rest on biography alone. It rests on access. In a factory built around shared breaks, open cups, sugar bowls, and casual habits, the route to harm did not require romance, family care, or a private dinner table. It only required patience, nearness, and a setting in which no one yet imagined that a co-worker might be using the break table as a delivery point.

The trust was thinner than intimacy, but it was still trust: colleagues expecting to get through the shift, finish a drink, and return to work. Sickness inside the workplace stopped looking random once investigators began linking repeated illnesses to what people were drinking.

Reports connected Young to poisonings delivered through tea and other workplace beverages, and the death of Fred Biggs gave the inquiry a fatal center. Thallium, rather than some vague workplace contaminant or passing medical mystery, became the substance around which the case tightened.

Once poison entered the explanation, the separate episodes of illness could be read together instead of one by one. The question was no longer whether several men at the factory had fallen mysteriously sick. It was whether one man had been dosing them over time under cover of routine.

## Evidence Trail

At trial, prosecutors presented a case built from convergence rather than spectacle. Toxic findings pointed to thallium. The pattern of repeated illness among Young's co-workers suggested a common route rather than unrelated bad luck. The timing of symptoms around drinks at work gave the prosecution a practical mechanism. And Young's own conduct, taken together with the wider sequence, was used to argue that these were deliberate administrations rather than accidental exposures.

The prosecution case said he had poisoned colleagues through tea and other drinks at the factory, with Fred Biggs's death standing as the clearest fatal result of that pattern. What makes the evidence so chilling in retrospect is how little theatrical staging it required. No forced entry, no dramatic confrontation, no scene that obviously announced itself as a murder scene.

The case was built by showing that a routine habit had become a repeatable delivery system and that the routine itself had helped conceal the harm.

## Courtroom Snapshot
Young was convicted in 1972 at St Albans Crown Court of murdering Fred Biggs and of poisoning or attempting to poison other co-workers. He received a life sentence. The conviction settled the legal core of the case, but it did not end the public argument around it. The question that echoed afterward was how someone with an earlier, known history of poisoning had been released from Broadmoor and allowed back into ordinary working life.

That concern appears directly in the House of Lords Hansard debate of June 29, 1972, where the case was discussed not simply as a murder conviction but as a failure of judgment about risk, release, and supervision. That aftermath matters because it shows why the case outlived the trial. It was remembered not only for poison in a teacup, but for the institutional question that followed the verdict. Young later died in custody in 1990.

## Case Takeaway
What lingers is not intimacy but routine. The Graham Young case depends not on family, romance, hospitality, or care, but on something colder: the unguarded trust of colleagues who simply expected to get through the day. Tea was not special. That was the point. It belonged to the shift, to the break, to the ordinary passing of time.

Once that ritual was turned into a method, the workplace stopped being just a workplace. It became a place where repetition itself helped hide intent until the pattern was too serious to dismiss.

---

**From poisoned tea in England, the story shifts to a family gathering in Brazil, where a Christmas table would become the center of devastating loss.**

**CASE 08 CITATIONS**

UK Parliament Hansard, 1972-06-29, The Case of Graham Young -- https://hansard.parliament.uk/lords/1972-06-29/debates/9388587f-1b45-45ee-8e0b-5456a6f4801e/TheCaseOfGrahamYoung

The Guardian, 2011-06-30, Archive: the release of psychopaths (1972) -- https://www.theguardian.com/theguardian/2011/jun/30/archive-the-release-of-psychopaths-1972

Wikipedia, Graham Young -- https://en.wikipedia.org/wiki/Graham_Young

## CASE 09

# CHRISTMAS CAKE CONTAMINATION

A family Christmas should have been marked by warmth and familiarity. Instead, this case follows how celebration gave way to grief when something deadly entered the food shared around the table.

## CHRISTMAS CAKE SPARKED ARSENIC CASE

### CASE DOSSIER

| | |
|---|---|
| Case subject: | Deise Moura dos Anjos |
| Location: | Torres, Rio Grande do Sul, Brazil |
| Key dates: | Dec. 23, 2024 \| Jan. 2025 \| Feb. 2025 |
| Victim(s): | Maida Berenice Flores da Silva \| Neuza Denize Silva dos Anjos \| Tatiana Denize Silva dos Santos \| three others survived |
| Method: | Arsenic-contaminated Christmas cake |
| Legal status: | Charged |
| Current posture: | Charged in 2025; died before trial, no verdict |

Slices were being passed around the table before anyone understood that the taste was the first sign something had gone badly wrong.

The gathering followed the ordinary rhythm of a family Christmas celebration. A festive family visit: coffee poured, cake cut, comments traded across the table, another bite taken almost automatically. Then someone noticed that the cake tasted strange. Reports later described it as peppery. That detail would become one of the most haunting parts of the case, because it captures the moment when warning arrived in the weakest possible form. The alarm did not come as smoke, collapse, or a visible contaminant. It came as taste, brief enough to question and easy enough to override inside a room built on familiarity.

Soon afterward, relatives who had eaten the cake began to fall violently ill. Hospital visits followed. Three women died. In the days after the gathering, investigators moved from a family table to toxicology labs, ingredient testing, and criminal charges. What makes this case land so hard is not only the scale of harm, but the shape of the object at its center. A Christmas cake is designed for sharing. It belongs to hospitality, repetition, and trust. In Torres, that shared object became the route by which suspicion, grief, and forensic scrutiny entered the room.

The case drew intense attention because the setting was intimate even before the losses became public. The gathering took place on December 23, 2024, during a family coffee visit in Torres, Rio Grande do Sul. Those who ate the cake included the woman who baked it, members of her immediate family, and a child. Reporting later noted that one person present did not eat the cake and did not become ill. The others who ate it began showing symptoms.

Three women died: two sisters, Maida Berenice Flores da Silva and Neuza Denize Silva dos Anjos, and Neuza's daughter, Tatiana Denize Silva dos Santos. Three others survived after hospitalization, including the baker. That pattern alone was enough to push investigators toward the table as the center of the case. But the pressure around the case widened quickly beyond the scene of serving. According to reports carried by CBS and CNN, investigators focused on Deise Moura dos Anjos, the daughter-in-law of the woman who baked the cake. By then, the public story had shifted from holiday tragedy to a possible attack inside a family already marked by tension.

Reports said police examined prior conflicts within the family as part of their motive theory. That helps explain why the case sits at the intersection of two familiar poisoning dynamics. One is practical: a shared food item, a common ingredient, a cluster of symptoms, and a toxicology trail that points back toward preparation. The other is relational: access shaped by family trust, where the ordinary act of accepting a slice carries none of the suspicion that a stranger's gift might.

Investigators did not stay long with the idea of ordinary spoilage. Once laboratory findings began to arrive, the case narrowed fast. Authorities said arsenic was detected in the victims' blood, in the remaining cake, and in the flour used to prepare it. That moved the case out of the realm of unexplained holiday illness and into forensic specificity.

The reported peppery taste became more disturbing in hindsight, because it marked the point at which the family sensed something was wrong without yet understanding the scale of danger. The baker reportedly told relatives to stop eating the cake, but by then the damage had already begun. What changed the case most sharply was the movement from the table to the ingredient. A shared dessert can leave investigators with many possible routes: filling, decoration, storage, utensils, last-minute contamination.

But once police and forensic analysts focused on the flour, the alleged act moved backward into preparation. Authorities reportedly said the arsenic concentration in that flour was so high that ordinary contamination could not explain it. From that point on, the case was no longer centered only on what had happened during the family visit. It was centered on how the poison, if intentionally introduced, entered the cake before it ever reached the table.

## Evidence Trail

The evidence in this case was unusually concentrated for a criminal proceeding that ended before trial. Authorities said expert analysis found arsenic at lethal levels in the victims' bodies. They also said remaining cake and the flour used to make it tested positive for arsenic, with reporting indicating that the flour concentration was vastly above permitted limits. That pattern offered investigators a common route that was both narrow and intelligible.

The same gathering produced the same emergency. The same dessert linked the victims. The same ingredient appeared again in the forensic chain.

Reporting carried by 9News from CNN said officials described the flour sample as containing arsenic at concentrations thousands of times above a permitted threshold. If accurate, that made an accidental explanation substantially harder to sustain. Police reportedly treated the flour as the decisive bridge between the physical symptoms in the room and the criminal allegations that followed.

Investigators also examined the broader context around the suspected contamination. Reports said police reviewed internet searches allegedly linked to arsenic and explored whether poison may have been acquired more than once. They also reopened scrutiny around an earlier family death, exhuming the baker's husband for testing as part of a wider inquiry. Those additional lines of investigation widened the atmosphere around the case, but they remained just that: lines of inquiry, not adjudicated findings.

The strongest evidentiary core stays closer to the December gathering itself: the cluster of illnesses, the three deaths, the survivors, the toxicology results, the cake, and the flour. Because the case stopped before trial, all of that remains part of the investigative and charging record rather than courtroom findings tested to verdict.

## Courtroom Snapshot

There was never a full courtroom sequence in the usual sense because the case did not reach trial. In January 2025, Brazilian police arrested Deise Moura dos Anjos and authorities filed charges alleging that she had contaminated the flour used in the Christmas cake with arsenic, causing three deaths and the poisoning of three surviving relatives. Reporting at the time reflected a prosecution theory built around intentional contamination during preparation rather than accidental poisoning at the table.

The defense posture, as reported publicly, was denial. She denied involvement in the poisonings. That left the case in a posture familiar to unresolved criminal proceedings: formal charges, substantial reported forensic evidence, and no adjudicated verdict.

Then the legal path ended abruptly. In February 2025, she was found dead in her jail cell while being held in pre-trial detention. Her death did not convert the allegations into proven fact, and it did not provide the courtroom testing that a trial would have supplied. It simply stopped the ordinary sequence by which the prosecution case would have been challenged, defended, and judged.

That is why the legal posture has to stay exact. There were charges. There was reported forensic evidence pointing toward arsenic contamination. There was no verdict. The criminal case likely ended with the suspect's death, even though related forensic or administrative inquiries could continue.

Under that posture, the allegations remained unproven in court at the time of her death, and she remained presumed innocent in law.

## Case Takeaway

This case stands out because the harm moved through an object designed to be divided. A Christmas cake is not private. It is cut, passed, accepted, and eaten in company. That shared form is what makes the case so disturbing. The same slices that expressed hospitality also appear, in the investigative record, as the route by which three women died and three others were hospitalized.

The toxicology, the flour analysis, and the formal charges create a strong investigative arc, but the case never reached the point where a court could test that arc against a defense at trial. The suspect's death in custody froze the record before the justice system completed its sequence.

So the case has to be held in two frames at once. In one frame, it is vivid and sharply specific: a family gathering, a strange taste, a rush to hospitals, arsenic in bodies, arsenic in cake, arsenic in flour. In the other, it remains legally unfinished. That combination is what gives the case its particular unease. The room is easy to imagine. The forensic route is easy to follow. But the final act of judgment never arrives.

---

**And where one family celebration turned fatal, the next case strips the method back even further, to a single milkshake that carried betrayal in plain sight.**

## CASE 09 CITATIONS

CBS News, January 6, 2025, "Woman arrested after arsenic-laced Christmas cake kills 3 family members in Brazil" -- https://www.cbsnews.com/news/arsenic-christmas-cake-deaths-woman-arrested-brazil/

9News, January 7, 2025, "Daughter-in-law arrested over Brazil Christmas cake poisonings" -- https://www.9news.com.au/world/brazil-christmas-cake-poisoning-arrest-arsenic-triple-homicide-crime-news/51dba0c8-bce1-498b-a2ed-dc3f682d4cba

People, February 14, 2025, "Woman accused of lacing Christmas cake with arsenic, killing 3, found dead in jail cell" -- https://people.com/woman-accused-lacing-cake-arsenic-killing-3-found-dead-jail-cell-11681143

## CASE 10

# MURDER BY MILKSHAKE

The betrayal at the heart of this case feels especially cruel because it arrived in such an innocent form, a familiar drink carrying consequences no one would suspect until it was too late.

## MILKSHAKE DELIVERY BECAME MURDER CASE

### CASE DOSSIER

| | |
|---|---|
| **Case subject:** | Rene Castellani |
| **Location:** | Vancouver, British Columbia, Canada |
| **Key dates:** | 1965 \| 1967 \| Jan. 1968 |
| **Victim(s):** | Esther Castellani |
| **Method:** | Arsenic-laced milkshake |
| **Legal status:** | Convicted |
| **Current posture:** | Death sentence was commuted to life imprisonment in 1968; later paroled |

A vanilla milkshake is supposed to feel harmless, even faintly indulgent. It arrives cold, sweet, and familiar. That is what makes the Rene Castellani case so disturbing.

In Vancouver in 1965, a drink associated with comfort and routine became the route for a slow arsenic murder. Esther Castellani grew seriously ill over weeks, not moments. Her decline did not announce itself as an obvious poisoning. It looked instead like sickness that would not settle into a diagnosis.

By the time the case was understood, the milkshake had stopped reading as a small kindness brought to hospital and started reading as a delivery system. What gives this case its force is not only the poison itself, but the patience of the method. The drink was ordinary. The doses were repeated. The violence hid inside something chosen because it seemed so easy to accept.

Rene Castellani was a well-known Vancouver radio promoter whose public image depended on charm, stunts, and attention. Behind that surface, sources describe an affair with Adelaide "Lolly" Miller, a receptionist connected to his work world, while Esther Castellani grew increasingly ill.

Contemporary and retrospective accounts frame the case around a motive that was both intimate and practical: a husband who wanted his wife gone so he could continue openly with another woman. That helps explain the case, but access is the bigger point. This was not a stranger's poisoning and not a public tampering case. It depended on the authority of a husband moving freely between home, hospital, and the routines of care.

Esther's favorite White Spot vanilla milkshakes became central to the later reconstruction because they were something she would reasonably accept from him without alarm. In a poisoning case, familiarity often does half the work before the poison ever enters the scene.

Suspicion hardened only after illness, death, and timing began to line up too closely to ignore. Esther died after weeks in Vancouver General Hospital. A doctor involved in her care kept looking at the symptoms and began to suspect arsenic rather than some obscure natural disease. That changed the shape of the case.

Hair analysis and the exhumation of Esther's body pointed investigators toward deliberate poisoning, and one detail became especially damaging: the poison pattern appeared to drop away during the period when Rene was highly visible atop the giant BowMac sign for a promotional stunt, then resume when that visibility ended. Once arsenic entered the explanation, the case no longer looked like unexplained decline inside a marriage. It looked like repeated dosing hidden inside routine visits and a favorite drink.

## Evidence Trail

The evidentiary path in this case was unusually concrete for a slow poisoning. The Canadian Encyclopedia and later retellings describe a suspicious doctor taking steps that led to toxic proof, while later summaries based on Eve Lazarus's reporting add the hospital timeline, the hair evidence, and the way the BowMac sign stunt created a visible gap in access.

Later accounts report that investigators found arsenic-containing weed killer under the kitchen sink, which they treated as the likely source tying means to method. As later summaries describe it, the prosecution relied on Esther's symptoms, toxic findings from hair and exhumation, a plausible milkshake delivery route, and surrounding circumstances to argue motive and opportunity, without needing a dramatic confession.

The case is a reminder that poison often builds its argument through accumulation: one symptom, then another, then a laboratory result, then an object in the house that suddenly reads very differently.

**Courtroom Snapshot**

Rene Castellani was charged, convicted of murder, and sentenced to death after trial in British Columbia. A federal inventory of Canadian death-penalty casefiles records Esther Castellani's killing as a 1965 Vancouver poisoning case, with trial proceedings in 1967 and commutation to life imprisonment by order in council in January 1968. Retrospective accounts agree on the legal core even when they differ in emphasis: the conviction fixed the murder in law, while the commutation kept the case inside Canada's late death-penalty era rather than ending at the gallows.

Later accounts also note that Castellani was eventually paroled. The central legal posture is the conviction, death sentence, and commutation to life. That sequence matters because it shows how seriously the court read the case: not as reckless neglect, but as deliberate homicidal poisoning.

## Case Takeaway

Poison can turn sweetness into camouflage. Nothing about the milkshake itself suggested danger. Its cold sweetness helped the method disappear into care, appetite, and habit. The route was not ceremonial, medicinal, or openly domestic in the old-fashioned sense. It was commercial, modern, familiar, and portable. A husband carried it in. A victim drank it. The proof came later.

---

**The next case returns to an American home, where a family meal and a later confession would reopen the story of a father's death in deeply unsettling ways.**

## CASE 10 CITATIONS

The Canadian Encyclopedia, 2019, Vancouver Feature: The Milkshake Murder -- https://www.thecanadianencyclopedia.ca/en/article/vancouver-feature-the-milkshake-murder

Government of Canada Publications, Persons Sentenced to Death in Canada, entry for Rene Emile Castellani -- https://publications.gc.ca/collections/collection_2017/bac-lac/SB4-46-1994-eng.pdf

Eve Lazarus, Cold Case Canada Podcast, Murder by Milkshake Part 2 -- https://evelazarus.com/cold-case-canada-podcast/s2-e23-murder-by-milkshake-part-2/

Vancouver Police Museum, Revisiting the Milkshake Murder -- https://www.vancouverpolicemuseum.ca/post/revisiting-the-milkshake-murder

72

## CASE 11

# TACO NIGHT CONFESSION

For years, a father's death seemed settled. Then a confession cracked the case open and turned one ordinary family dinner into the starting point of a far more troubling story.

## TACO DİNNER REOPENED DEATH CASE

**CASE DOSSIER**

| | |
|---|---|
| **Case subject:** | Marie Robards |
| **Location:** | Fort Worth, Texas, USA |
| **Key dates:** | Feb. 17-18, 1993 \| Oct. 1994 \| 1996 Jan. 29, 1998 |
| **Victim(s):** | Steven Robards |
| **Method:** | Barium-laced tacos |
| **Legal status:** | Convicted |
| **Current posture:** | Conviction affirmed in 1998; later released on parole in 2003 |

The dinner had already been eaten by the time Steven Robards began vomiting. Tacos had been made from refried beans served at home in Fort Worth.

What followed moved fast: violent illness, collapse, emergency help, and death within hours. At first, the scene looked like a sudden domestic medical crisis with no clear criminal shape. His death was ruled a heart attack, and the meal disappeared with the ordinary logic of a family dinner that had already ended.

What makes the case linger is how much of it seemed settled before it ever really began. The plate was gone. The kitchen had gone quiet. The family story made enough sense to hold. Even at the funeral, the future she thought she wanted was already taking shape beyond the death. That fact would only sharpen the cruelty of what prosecutors later said had happened at the table.

Marie Robards was sixteen when her father died. Reporting at the time and later accounts described a family arrangement shaped by divorce, remarriage, and conflict over where she would live. Prosecutors later argued that she wanted out of her father's home and believed his death would clear the path back to her mother. The motive they presented was brutally simple, but the household itself was more complicated than a courtroom summary could hold.

She was described as a bright student. Steven Robards was a father trying to manage ordinary life after a broken marriage. Nothing about the setting suggested spectacle. This was a weekday meal in an apartment kitchen, a parent, a daughter, and a frustration that stayed private until it was forced into the open. Later accounts added the detail that, at Steven's funeral, Marie learned her mother had already planned to leave her stepfather and move with her anyway.

Prosecutors used that fact to underscore how unnecessary the killing had been, even on its own terms.

More than a year after Steven Robards died, a secret left the room where it had been kept. Marie told a friend she had poisoned her father. The friend carried that confession for a time, then went to a school counselor, and the counselor took it to police. A death that had been folded into the past no longer sat still.

That disclosure changed the meaning of everything that came before it. Investigators reopened a case that had already been explained, buried, and grieved. The central question was no longer whether Steven Robards had died suddenly. It was whether he had been killed at his own dinner table and whether the answer had been sitting, unnoticed, inside the original record all along.

## Evidence Trail

According to charging and trial reporting, detectives learned that Marie had stolen barium acetate from a bottle in her high school chemistry classroom and concealed it in a napkin. The dinner details are consistently described as a Mexican meal: she mixed the chemical into refried beans, and Steven used those beans to make tacos before becoming violently ill.

Preserved samples were tested again, and the toxicology pointed to acute barium intoxication rather than a natural collapse. Prosecutors used that result to rebuild the night in reverse: the school chemical, the beans, the symptoms, the death. After her arrest, Marie confessed to police.

At trial, she maintained that she had only meant to make her father sick, not kill him. By then, the evidence had given the meal a much harder outline. The source of the poison was unusually concrete, and the old samples had survived long enough to contradict the first ruling.

## Courtroom Snapshot

The state charged Dorothy Marie Robards in October 1994 after the reinvestigation turned a presumed natural death into a homicide case. She was ultimately tried as an adult in Tarrant County. Prosecutors argued that she had poisoned her father's food with a chemical taken from school because she wanted out of the living arrangement and believed his death would solve that problem. The defense, as later accounts summarized it, leaned on lack of intent to kill and on her youth.

A jury convicted her of murder in 1996 and sentenced her to 27 years in prison, though some later accounts say 28. Her appeal was affirmed on January 29, 1998. Marie Robards was later released on parole in 2003 after serving about seven years. Whatever complexities surrounded the household, the legal record fixed the dinner as murder rather than accident.

## Case Takeaway

What lingers in the Robards case is the delay. The poisoning was not exposed by an immediate forensic triumph or by a dramatic scene at the hospital. It surfaced because a teenage confession reached a friend, then a counselor, then the police, and because the old samples had not been lost.

That sequence is what made the case endure. The meal itself was ordinary enough to vanish into the first explanation. Only later did the case harden into something else: a family dinner re-read as homicide, a father's death reopened by words, and a teenager forced back toward the night she thought had already passed behind her.

---

**From one family dinner in Texas, the scale widens sharply. Next comes a case that spread fear across Japan, proving that poisoned drinks could unsettle an entire country.**

## CASE 11 CITATIONS

UPI Archives, 1994-10-19, Student charged with poisoning her dad -- https://www.upi.com/Archives/1994/10/19/Student-charged-with-poisoning-her-dad/7014782539200/

Texas Monthly, 1996-07, Poisoning Daddy -- https://www.texasmonthly.com/articles/poisoning-daddy/

Wikipedia, Marie Robards -- https://en.wikipedia.org/wiki/Marie_Robards

Justia, 1998-01-29, Robards, Dorothy Marie v. The State of Texas -- https://law.justia.com/cases/texas/second-court-of-appeals/1998/?page=3

78

## CASE 12

# THE VENDING MACHINE PANIC

This case widens from individual victims to national dread, showing how public convenience and casual trust were exploited in a poisoning wave that left fear sitting in plain sight.

## BOTTLES BY MACHINES SPARKED PANIC

---

### CASE DOSSIER

| | |
|---|---|
| **Case subject:** | 1985 paraquat vending machine poisoner |
| **Location:** | Japan |
| **Key dates:** | 1985 |
| **Victim(s):** | About 10 known deaths reported in the 1985 series |
| **Method:** | Paraquat-laced drinks left near vending machines |
| **Legal status:** | Unsolved |
| **Current posture:** | No offender was publicly identified |

---

The bottle was not purchased in the usual way. That small detail helped explain the method.

In Japan in 1985, drinks later found to be fatal were discovered sitting on or near vending machines, left there as if someone had simply forgotten them or decided not to finish. That small break in routine became the mechanism of the case. A passerby could see a sealed or unattended drink, assume it had been abandoned, and pick it up without thinking much about it. What followed turned a familiar piece of urban infrastructure into a source of dread. The danger was not in the machine itself. It was in the bottle waiting just beside it.

This case does not center on marriage, family grievance, or one relationship under strain. It belongs to public space. Vending machines are built around trust in systems rather than trust in people. You expect the product to be standardized, untouched, and safe. The paraquat poisonings exploited that expectation by sitting just outside the machine's normal transaction logic. The pressure in the case comes from social habit. People knew how to behave around vending machines. The killer appears to have counted on that.

The poisoning pattern became clear as contaminated soft drinks were linked across multiple incidents. UPI reported that Japanese authorities warned the public not to pick up drinks left on or near vending machines after a series of deaths tied to paraquat. Once that warning went public, the pattern was unmistakable. These were not random medical collapses spread by coincidence. They were linked by route, by object, and by the unsettling simplicity of the delivery method. The city itself changed shape. A bottle that might once have looked like luck or waste now looked like a trap.

## Evidence Trail

Investigators and later commentators describe the evidence as sufficient to establish a clear poisoning pattern, but not sufficient to identify and prosecute a specific offender. That combination is what gives the case its staying power. UPI reported that ten people had been killed and that the poison was paraquat, a highly toxic herbicide. Authorities understood the route and the broad method. What they did not secure, at least publicly, was the person behind it.

Reports also noted dozens of suspected tampering incidents, many non-fatal, which helped drive nationwide fear of abandoned drinks near vending machines. The bottles, the locations, and the toxic findings created the case. The missing defendant is part of the case's shape, not a flaw in it.

## Courtroom Snapshot

There is no courtroom verdict to anchor this case because the paraquat vending machine poisonings remained unsolved. The legal posture is investigative and historical rather than adjudicated. What can be stated firmly is the route described in the reporting: poisoned bottled drinks left near vending machines, public warnings issued, and multiple deaths attributed to paraquat. The case closes not with sentence or appeal, but with a public still waiting for a defendant who never appeared in the record.

## Case Takeaway

A vending machine is supposed to remove uncertainty. You insert money, choose a drink, and receive something standardized.

The paraquat case worked by hovering just outside that promise. The bottle was not inside the machine. It was close enough to trade on the machine's aura of safety. That is what made the panic spread. A drink sitting in plain sight, in a city learning not to trust it, is one of the starkest images a poisoning case can leave behind.

---

**The next case closes that public distance again, returning to the intimacy of marriage, where an anniversary meal concealed a much more deliberate threat.**

## CASE 12 CITATIONS

UPI Archives, 1985-10-27, Beverage poisonings kill 10 in Japan -- https://www.upi.com/Archives/1985/10/27/Beverage-poisonings-kill-10-in-Japan/5516499233600/

UPI Archives, 1985-09-27, Japanese warned against poisoned soft drinks -- https://www.upi.com/Archives/1985/09/27/Japanese-warned-against-poisoned-soft-drinks/9882496641600/

Wikipedia, Paraquat murders -- https://en.wikipedia.org/wiki/Paraquat_murders

## CASE 13

# ANNIVERSARY DINNER TRAP

An occasion meant to celebrate love instead became a setting for suspicion, toxic intent, and a meal prosecutors said was part of a plan already taking shape behind closed doors.

**ANNIVERSARY DINNER BECAME MURDER TRAP**

### CASE DOSSIER

| | |
|---|---|
| **Case subject:** | Kate Knight |
| **Location:** | Stoke-on-Trent area, Staffordshire, UK |
| **Key dates:** | Apr. 2005 \| Jan. 29, 2008 \| Feb. 28, 2008 |
| **Victim(s):** | Lee Knight |
| **Method:** | Antifreeze-laced food and wine |
| **Legal status:** | Convicted |
| **Current posture:** | Sentenced in 2008; 30-year term later upheld on appeal |

The table was set for an anniversary dinner, not an attempted murder trial. There was red wine, takeaway curry, and the kind of private domestic quiet that usually disappears from memory as soon as the evening ends.

Nothing about it suggested catastrophe. That is part of what makes the Kate Knight case so hard to shake. Prosecutors said the food and wine served on that seventh wedding anniversary carried ethylene glycol, the toxic chemical found in antifreeze. Lee Knight did not collapse in some public spectacle. He became gravely ill after the meal and entered a prolonged medical crisis that left him blind, partly deaf, brain injured, and catastrophically injured.

The scene did not announce itself as violence while it was happening. It looked like a shared meal between husband and wife, which is exactly what made it such an effective setting for concealment.

Kate and Lee Knight were a married couple in the Stoke-on-Trent area with a young son and a household that still looked, from the outside, like something holding together. In court, prosecutors said that appearance concealed severe financial strain.

Reporting from the trial said Kate Knight had taken out loans in her husband's name by forging his signature and hoped that money linked to his death, including employment-related benefits, would solve mounting debts. That financial pressure mattered because it gave the prosecution a motive that was both practical and cold.

The defense offered a different picture. Knight denied poisoning her husband and said the marriage had been unhappy and violent.

But even with those competing accounts in play, the center of the case remained brutally simple: this was a private domestic setting in which access was easy, suspicion was low, and the person receiving the meal had no reason to treat the table in front of him as dangerous.

What changed the case was not a dramatic public collapse but the growing recognition that the anniversary meal itself was the delivery system. Prosecutors told Stafford Crown Court that Kate Knight had put ethylene glycol into both the red wine and the curry served on April 14, 2005.

The court also heard evidence that she had considered other ways of killing her husband before settling on antifreeze, including overdosing him with ecstasy or iron tablets. That evidence gave the serving its full meaning. The dinner no longer looked like a domestic ritual that ended in unexplained sickness. It looked, in the prosecution case later accepted by the jury, like a planned attempt to kill a husband in his own home using food and drink ordinary enough to pass without challenge.

## Evidence Trail

The prosecution case was built from toxicology, motive, and one chilling piece of witness evidence that turned private suspicion into something far harder to dismiss. Doctors eventually linked Lee Knight's condition to ethylene glycol poisoning. The damage was immense. He spent weeks in a coma and was left blind, partly deaf, brain damaged, and with catastrophic kidney injury. Later reporting made clear that he required ongoing full-time care and lost the working life he had before the poisoning.

Investigators also presented a financial motive. Prosecutors said Knight had hidden debts, forged her husband's signature on loans, and hoped to benefit from his death. But the detail that gives the case its sharpest edge came from a neighbor.

She told the court that Knight showed her wine and antifreeze under the sink, said she had put antifreeze in her husband's curry and wine, and later said "it's worked" after Lee Knight had been admitted to hospital. That evidence helped transform the case from poisoning inferred by chemistry alone into one supported by alleged preparation, admission, and aftermath.

The jury heard not just that a toxin had been found, but that the poisoning fit inside a pattern of debt, planning, concealment, and a remark that sounded like satisfaction once the harm was already underway.

## Courtroom Snapshot

Kate Knight denied trying to murder her husband, but on January 29, 2008 a jury at Stafford Crown Court found her guilty of attempted murder. Prosecutors said she had deliberately laced Lee Knight's wine and curry with antifreeze in order to kill him and gain financially.

The defense denied deliberate poisoning and raised claims of an unhappy, violent marriage. The jury accepted the prosecution case.

On February 28, 2008, the court sentenced Knight to 30 years' imprisonment, less 30 days already served on remand, with a minimum term of 15 years before she could be considered for release. The judge treated the offense as a carefully planned attempt to murder for financial gain, made more serious by the scale of the injuries Lee Knight survived.

Her sentence was later upheld by the Court of Appeal, which rejected the argument that it was manifestly excessive. Legally, the case is settled. The poisoning was charged, contested, proved, punished, and affirmed on appeal as attempted murder.

## Case Takeaway

This case is hard to forget because it turns an anniversary into a weapon. A shared dinner is supposed to mark loyalty, routine, and private history. Here, the same domestic setting became the means of administration. That contrast gives the case its force, but the deeper impact comes from duration.

The poisoning happened in one evening. The damage stretched through intensive care, permanent disability, trial, sentence, and appeal. It also shows how an ingestion case can be built from a mixture of quiet elements that, on their own, might seem almost ordinary: a meal, a bottle under a sink, hidden debt, a witness who finally speaks, and a body that never returns to what it was. Nothing in that list looks theatrical. Together, it becomes devastating.

**But domestic poisoning did not always arrive with obvious drama. In the next case, repeated deaths inside one household slowly turned grief into suspicion.**

## CASE 13 CITATIONS

Court of Appeal (Criminal Division), Regina v Knight -- https://www.casemine.com/judgement/uk/5b46f2072c94e0775e7f0c57

Court of Appeal (Criminal Division), Knight, R v -- https://www.casemine.com/judgement/uk/6521ad562cec034620af1782

Evening Standard, My wife poisoned me with anti-freeze, then tried to finish me off -- https://www.standard.co.uk/hp/front/my-wife-poisoned-me-with-antifreeze-then-tried-to-finish-me-off-as-i-fought-for-life-in-hospital-7288550.html

Evening Standard, Woman who poisoned husband with antifreeze to clear her debts -- https://www.standard.co.uk/hp/front/woman-who-poisoned-husband-with-antifreeze-to-clear-her-debts-enquired-after-hitman-6686638.html

## CASE 14

# THE DEATHS IN DERBY

This case is driven by accumulation: not one alarming moment, but a series of losses that slowly transformed sorrow into suspicion, and suspicion into one of the era's defining poison cases.

## DERBY HOUSEHOLD MEALS CARRIED ARSENIC

### CASE DOSSIER

| | |
|---|---|
| **Case subject:** | Lydia Sherman |
| **Location:** | Derby, Connecticut, USA |
| **Key dates:** | 1860s-early 1870s \| 1872 |
| **Victim(s):** | Horatio Sherman in the conviction case \| multiple earlier family members also linked in later accounts |
| **Method:** | Arsenic poisoning through food and drink |
| **Legal status:** | Convicted |
| **Current posture:** | Sentenced to life imprisonment in 1872; died in custody in 1878 |

Grief arrived in the Lydia Sherman case before suspicion did. In a Connecticut household, illness and death could still be absorbed into the accepted language of misfortune, especially when they passed through meals, medicine, and the daily work of care. That is what made the case so difficult to read at first.

Nothing about the setting forced an immediate criminal interpretation. The danger sat inside domestic habit, where a wife and mother could move between tending, serving, and mourning without appearing to step outside her role.

Lydia Sherman lived inside the expected nineteenth-century role of wife, mother, and household caretaker, and that role shaped the case against her. Retrospective accounts would later cast her as one of America's earliest notorious female poisoners, but the legal record is narrower than the legend. Even so, the pattern around her was difficult to ignore.

Multiple husbands, children, and stepchildren died over time in circumstances later associated with arsenic, and investigators gradually stopped treating those losses as isolated family tragedy. Horatio Sherman, whose death anchored the conviction case, was the final point at which private bereavement gave way to public scrutiny.

The pressure in the case came from accumulation. Each death on its own could be received as grief. Taken together, they began to look like method.

Suspicion stopped attaching to grief and began attaching to the person moving through it. Authorities and contemporary reporting focused on arsenic and on the clustered deaths of husbands and children around Sherman. Once that happened, prosecutors framed the case on the idea that the home had provided both access and cover. The household setting did not weaken the prosecution. It explained how poison could be introduced without spectacle and why the case had remained readable as misfortune for so long.

## Evidence Trail

The evidentiary force of the Sherman case came from pattern, access, and the belief that arsenic had been repeatedly available inside the home. Historic reporting tied her to multiple deaths, but the case has to separate reputation from the harder legal core.

The law eventually secured a conviction tied to one principal murder count, while public understanding, shaped by period reports and later writers, widened to include a longer chain of suspected family victims. Horatio Sherman therefore needs to remain visible in the narrative, not just in the dossier, because his death is where suspicion finally hardened into a courtroom result.

Later accounts also tied arsenic findings to other exhumed bodies connected to the household, which helped prosecutors and reporters argue that the pattern was larger than one bereavement. That distinction matters. Not every death later attributed to Sherman can be treated as one clean courtroom tally.

The stronger claim is the narrower one: repeated suspicion, arsenic, clustered family deaths, and a conviction that turned accumulated loss into legal fact.

## Courtroom Snapshot

Lydia Sherman was convicted in 1872 and sentenced to life imprisonment at Wethersfield State Prison. Contemporary and later historical summaries treat the prosecution as a case built on arsenic, domestic access, and a pattern of deaths that had become too concentrated to dismiss.

Horatio Sherman's death supplied the principal murder count, even while broader suspicion extended to earlier husbands and children. Sherman later escaped briefly from prison in 1877 under the pretext of illness, was recaptured, and was returned to Wethersfield. She died there in 1878.

The legal posture is firm even if the total victim count is not. There was a real conviction, a real life sentence, and a real prison record. The wider chain remains partly a matter of period reporting and retrospective reconstruction.

## Case Takeaway

What endures is not simply arsenic but the way grief itself functioned as camouflage. A household can absorb one death into sympathy. It can sometimes absorb a second into bad luck. A longer pattern forces a different reading. In the Sherman case, meals, medicines, and caretaking were not dramatic props.

They were the ordinary instruments through which trust could be used and reused without immediate alarm. That is why the case lasts in the historical record. The setting is familiar. The repetition is what turns it from sorrow into suspicion.

---

**From a Connecticut household, the story moves to one of the most infamous public poisonings of the modern era, where a teapot in London carried consequences far beyond the table.**

## CASE 14 CITATIONS

Murder by Gaslight, historical summary of Lydia Sherman and the Derby poisonings -- https://www.murderbygaslight.com/2010/02/lydia-sherman-derby-poisoner.html

Connecticut History, "Lydia Sherman: The Derby Poisoner" -- https://connecticuthistory.org/lydia-sherman-the-derby-poisoner/

New England Historical Society, summary of the Sherman case, exhumations, trial, and death in prison -- https://newenglandhistoricalsociety.com/lydia-sherman-the-derby-poisoner-commits-the-horror-of-the-century/

# JAMES HAMPSTEAD

## CASE 15

# THE RADIOACTIVE TEAPOT

The object at the center of this case was almost absurdly ordinary, which only sharpened the horror when investigators discovered that one of the world's most notorious poisons had passed across the table.

## HOTEL TEA BECAME RADIOACTIVE EVIDENCE

### CASE DOSSIER

| | |
|---|---|
| **Case subject:** | Alexander Litvinenko |
| **Location:** | London, England, UK |
| **Key dates:** | Nov. 1 & Nov. 23, 2006 \| Jan. 21, 2016 |
| **Victim(s):** | Alexander Litvinenko |
| **Method:** | Polonium-210 in tea |
| **Legal status:** | No UK trial verdict |
| **Current posture:** | Public inquiry concluded in 2016 that Russian agents poisoned Litvinenko; no UK criminal trial result against them |

The tea did not look different from any other cup served in a London hotel bar. A white teapot on a small table in the Millennium Hotel should have belonged to routine conversation, not to one of the most notorious poisonings of the modern era.

When Alexander Litvinenko met Andrei Lugovoi and Dmitry Kovtun on November 1, 2006, the setting was quiet enough to feel forgettable. The danger was not. By the time he became violently ill later that day, the cup had already become the center of a murder case whose contamination trail would spread across hotels, offices, aircraft, hospitals, and finally into a public inquiry.

Litvinenko was a former Russian security officer living in Britain and openly critical of the Kremlin. The wider political background cannot be ignored, but the case works best when it stays close to the meeting itself.

The case is not powered by a domestic argument or a collapsing marriage. It is driven by a targeted encounter in a public setting where the victim had reason to believe he was attending a meeting, not walking into a radiological attack.

What made the room dangerous was not the setting alone, but the familiarity of the people inside it. This was not a random poisoning. It was a directed one, built around who would sit down, who would pour, and who would drink.

Litvinenko fell ill almost immediately after the meeting, with vomiting and severe gastric symptoms. At first, the cause was far from obvious. What transformed the case was the eventual discovery of polonium-210 in his body and at multiple sites connected to the suspects' movements.

Once polonium entered the record, the meeting at the hotel stopped looking like an ordinary tea and became the critical event in a much larger reconstruction. The question was no longer whether he had been poisoned. It was when, where, and by whom.

## Evidence Trail

The evidentiary record in this case is exceptionally detailed for a case that never reached trial. The UK public inquiry and public-health reports described extensive polonium-210 contamination across multiple London locations, including sites linked to the November 1 meeting.

The inquiry concluded that Litvinenko ingested polonium in tea served from a teapot at the Millennium Hotel. That finding tied the route of harm to a specific public setting and method.

The Health Protection Agency's later monitoring report also showed how unusual the case was: contamination had to be traced not only around the victim, but around the wider urban path the poison had taken. This was not simply a murder case. It was a radiological incident mapped through a city.

## Courtroom Snapshot

There was no British criminal trial that produced a verdict against Lugovoi and Kovtun. Instead, the legal and public conclusion came through the Litvinenko Inquiry, a statutory public inquiry chaired by Sir Robert Owen and published in January 2016.

The case does not end with a conviction. It ends with a formal state inquiry finding that Lugovoi and Kovtun poisoned Litvinenko and that the operation was probably approved at senior levels of the Russian state. The inquiry carried major formal weight, but it was still an inquiry finding rather than a jury verdict. The case therefore belongs in the category of inquiry-based conclusion, not courtroom conviction, even though the evidentiary record is exceptionally detailed.

## Case Takeaway

Tea should have made the meeting look harmless. Instead, it gave the attack its camouflage. A hotel teapot belongs to hospitality, business, and routine courtesy, which is precisely why it could conceal something as extreme as polonium-210 long enough for the poison to do its work. What makes the Litvinenko case so singular is that the contamination did not stay inside one cup or one room. It spread outward into hotels, offices, aircraft, hospitals, and finally into a statutory public inquiry. The route was intimate. The evidentiary footprint became metropolitan, then geopolitical.

**The next case returns to Australia, where hospitality, trust, and a carefully prepared lunch would become the center of one of the most disturbing modern allegations in the collection.**

## CASE 15 CITATIONS

GOV.UK, The Litvinenko inquiry: report into the death of Alexander Litvinenko -- https://www.gov.uk/government/publications/the-litvinenko-inquiry-report-into-the-death-of-alexander-litvinenko

GOV.UK, Polonium-210: individual monitoring after an incident -- https://www.gov.uk/government/publications/polonium-210-individual-monitoring-after-an-incident

Reuters, archival coverage summarized in public reporting on the 2016 inquiry findings

## CASE 16

# A TABLE SET FOR BETRAYAL

Few meals have attracted as much dread as this one, where a carefully prepared lunch became the focus of allegations so shocking they pulled family trust, hospitality, and death into the same frame.

## BEEF WELLINGTON LUNCH TURNED DEADLY

### CASE DOSSIER

| | |
|---|---|
| **Case subject:** | Erin Patterson |
| **Location:** | Leongatha, Victoria, Australia |
| **Key dates:** | July 29, 2023 \| July 7, 2025 \| Sept. 8, 2025 |
| **Victim(s):** | Gail Patterson \| Don Patterson \| Heather Wilkinson \| Ian Wilkinson (survived) |
| **Method:** | Death cap mushrooms in Beef Wellington |
| **Legal status:** | Convicted |
| **Current posture:** | Sentenced in 2025 to life imprisonment with a 33-year non-parole period; appeal filings pending at draft date |

The meal was built to look careful. Beef Wellington is not an improvised lunch. It suggests planning, portions, timing, and a host who wants the table to feel considered. Pastry, mushrooms, mashed potato, green beans, family conversation in regional Victoria. Nothing in the scene announced panic. Everything in it suggested effort.

That surface normality is what gave the Erin Patterson case its force. On July 29, 2023, four lunch guests ate at Patterson's home in Leongatha. Gail Patterson, Don Patterson, Heather Wilkinson, and Ian Wilkinson all became gravely ill. Gail, Don, and Heather later died. Ian survived after weeks in hospital. By the time the legal record settled into counts, verdicts, and sentence, the central image had never changed: a family lunch that looked orderly right up until it became catastrophic.

The power of the case does not come from spectacle. It comes from compression. A private meal produced a tightly bounded question set: who was invited, who attended, what was served, what the host ate, what she said afterward, and whether the poisoned mushrooms could plausibly have entered the meal by mistake.

When the jury convicted Patterson in July 2025 of three murders and one attempted murder, it did not transform the scene into something gothic. It confirmed that, in the prosecution's account, the danger had been placed inside a setting built to feel safe.

The emotional pressure in this case was fixed by the guest list before any courtroom argument began. These were not strangers gathered by coincidence. Gail and Don Patterson were Patterson's former parents-in-law. Heather Wilkinson was Gail's sister. Ian Wilkinson was Heather's husband and a local pastor. Simon Patterson, Erin Patterson's estranged husband, had also been invited, but did not attend. That absence later became one of the details the public kept circling back to, because the lunch was never just a meal. It was a deliberately limited social event.

What made the case especially disturbing was that the invitation appeared, at least on its face, to belong to the ordinary grammar of family repair. Meals are often used to smooth strain, mark civility, or reopen contact. Prosecutors did not need to prove a melodramatic feud to make the lunch count as more than hospitality. They needed jurors to sit with the fact that hospitality itself may have been used as the delivery route. There was pressure in the relationships, pressure in the deaths, and pressure in the visibility of the aftermath.

When several people fall ill after the same meal, the social script changes instantly. What did everyone eat? Did the host eat the same thing? When did symptoms begin? A shared lunch becomes a collective timeline. In this case, Ian Wilkinson's survival gave that timeline a living witness, and the prosecution later used the narrowness of the guest group and the specificity of the meal to argue that chance had very little room left inside it.

The lunch stopped looking like background and became the entire map. In the first hours of serious illness, a home-cooked meal can still belong to the world of tragic accident. Families, doctors, and investigators often start with the ordinary explanation because most shared meals do not conceal criminal intent. But once death cap poisoning entered the picture, the field of possible explanations narrowed sharply.

From that point on, the central issue was no longer simply what had made everyone sick. It was how Amanita phalloides had entered a lunch served to four specific guests and whether that could be explained as a mistake. Patterson's position was that the deaths were accidental. Prosecutors said the contamination was deliberate. That conflict gave every small detail unusual weight. Portioning took on significance. So did plate comparisons. What Patterson said about mushroom sourcing became important. Later conduct mattered too, including evidence surrounding the dehydrator that investigators linked to mushroom traces.

Poison cases often change shape quietly. There is not always a dramatic eyewitness moment that splits the story in two. Sometimes the decisive movement is the collapse of innocent ambiguity. That is what happened here. Once toxicology, medical evidence, guest selection, and post-lunch conduct were read together, the case no longer looked like a mystery about what substance had caused the harm. It became a dispute about whether the harm had been planned.

## Evidence Trail

The prosecution case was built as a chain rather than a single revelation. Reuters reported that Patterson served individual Beef Wellingtons with mashed potato and green beans at her Leongatha lunch on July 29, 2023. All four guests became seriously ill.

Three died. Ian Wilkinson survived. The toxic core of the case was the presence of death cap mushrooms, but that finding did not answer intent by itself. The trial therefore turned on surrounding conduct and on whether Patterson's explanations could be believed.

Reuters and ABC reported that prosecutors argued Patterson had lied about important matters, including mushroom foraging and ownership of a dehydrator. Police later recovered a dehydrator from a nearby dump, and testing identified material consistent with death cap mushrooms.

Prosecutors also alleged Patterson fabricated a cancer claim to help secure the lunch, served herself a different portion, and took steps after the meal that pointed away from accident and toward concealment. Patterson denied deliberately poisoning anyone and said she had lied about some matters out of embarrassment, including over weight-loss surgery, not because she had planned a murder.

That evidentiary structure carried the case because no witness claimed to have seen poison added to the food and no confession arrived to settle the story.

Jurors had to decide whether the full accumulation, including toxicology, contradictions, disposal evidence, selective explanations, and the narrow guest list, made accident implausible.

In circumstantial poisoning cases, the chain is the argument. Here, the chain was strong enough to support convictions on all four counts.

## Courtroom Snapshot

The trial was heard in the Supreme Court of Victoria sitting at Morwell and ran for about ten weeks in 2025. Prosecutors argued that Patterson had deliberately served lunch containing death cap mushrooms to Gail Patterson, Don Patterson, Heather Wilkinson, and Ian Wilkinson.

The defense said Patterson had lied about some surrounding matters but had not intended to poison anyone, and that the deaths were a terrible accident.

Patterson gave evidence in her own defense, which pushed credibility to the center of the case. Jurors were asked to weigh not only toxicology and timeline evidence, but also her account of the cancer lie, the mushroom sourcing, and the discarded dehydrator.

On July 7, 2025, the jury found her guilty of three counts of murder and one count of attempted murder. On September 8, 2025, Justice Christopher Beale sentenced her to life imprisonment with a non-parole period of 33 years.

The case remains active at the appeal stage. ABC News reported in October 2025 that prosecutors appealed the sentence as manifestly inadequate, and in November 2025 that Patterson lodged appeal documents challenging her convictions. Those appeal steps do not alter the central trial record. A jury heard weeks of evidence, accepted the prosecution case, and returned guilty verdicts. What remains open is the appellate path, not the fact that this lunch has already been judged in court as a deliberate poisoning.

## Case Takeaway

The lunch was not simply where the harm occurred. It was the delivery system, the guest filter, the timeline, and the reason the prosecution could build its argument through narrowing rather than spectacle. Poison arrived dressed as care. A home-cooked dish, a dessert plate, a drink prepared in private, a snack set out without warning: the setting asks for trust before it asks for fear. That is why ingestion cases feel different from stranger violence. The threat is embedded in hospitality itself.

The Patterson case also shows how little room remains for coincidence once a served item becomes the center of a complete evidentiary chain. Invitation, meal, collapse, toxicology, contradiction, verdict. The sequence is brutally compact. Nothing about the room needed to look sinister. The danger did not stand outside the table. It was placed on it.

---

**From mushrooms at the family table, the story shifts back in time and across the world, to a homemade drink in rural Canada and a case shaped by suspicion close to home.**

## CASE 16 CITATIONS

Reuters, 2025-07-07, Australian Erin Patterson found guilty in mushroom murders case -- https://www.reuters.com/business/media-telecom/australian-erin-patterson-found-guilty-all-counts-mushroom-murders-case-2025-07-07/

Reuters, 2025-09-08, Australia mushroom murderer Erin Patterson jailed minimum 33 years -- https://www.reuters.com/business/media-telecom/australia-mushroom-murderer-erin-patterson-jailed-minimum-33-years-2025-09-08/

ABC News (AU), 2025-09-08, Mushroom murderer Erin Patterson sentenced to life in prison -- https://www.abc.net.au/news/2025-09-08/mushroom-murderer-erin-patterson-sentenced-to-life-in-prison/105735360

Supreme Court of Victoria, 2025, DPP v PATTERSON [2025] VSC 557 sentence summary -- https://www.supremecourt.vic.gov.au/areas/case-summaries/recent-sentences

ABC News (AU), 2025-10-06, Director of Public Prosecutions to appeal Erin Patterson's sentence -- https://www.abc.net.au/news/2025-10-06/dpp-appeal-erin-patterson-sentence/105858980

ABC News (AU), 2025-11-05, Convicted mushroom murderer Erin Patterson outlines her reasons to appeal -- https://www.abc.net.au/news/2025-11-05/erin-patterson-mushroom-murderer-appeals-conviction/105975896

## CASE 17

# HOMEMADE POWDERED DRINK

A drink mixed at home became the focal point of a case built on suspicion close to the family circle, where strychnine turned something simple into something fatal.

## POWDERED DRINK CARRIED STRYCHNINE

### CASE DOSSIER

| | |
|---|---|
| **Case subject:** | Michael MacKay |
| **Location:** | Meota/Battleford, Saskatchewan, Canada |
| **Key dates:** | Feb. 2020 \| Nov. 2023 |
| **Victim(s):** | Cindy MacKay |
| **Method:** | Strychnine-poisoned homemade drink |
| **Legal status:** | Convicted |
| **Current posture:** | Pleaded guilty in 2023 to second-degree murder; life sentence with no parole for 10 years |

The drink was meant to feel helpful before it felt wrong. On a cold February morning in rural Saskatchewan, Cindy MacKay was unwell at home while her husband handled the ordinary movements of the day: children dressed, lunches packed, school run made. When he returned, he mixed her a drink with powdered Gatorade. It looked like care in a glass. Prosecutors would later argue it was the delivery route for strychnine.

Michael and Cindy MacKay had been married for years, had children, and were living on her family's farm near Meota, northwest of Battleford. Reporting on the later court proceedings described the marriage as strained and MacKay as frustrated with his life. An agreed statement of facts said Michael MacKay had started an affair in the months before Cindy died, and court heard he had been carrying long-running mental health struggles. None of that changed the object at the center of the case. This was not a hidden vial, a lab setup, or a staged scene. It was a drink mixed inside the home and handed over as though it belonged to the routine of a sick day. That domestic context matters because it lowered resistance. A powdered drink prepared by a spouse does not look like a weapon. It looks like practical care.

Medical staff treated the death as suspicious, and investigators connected the physical symptoms to poisoning. Strychnine is not subtle. Court heard Cindy noticed the drink tasted wrong and brushed her teeth, but the poison's effects took over quickly. Her muscles began contracting violently and painfully.

She went into cardiac arrest during the ambulance ride and later died in hospital from multiple organ failure caused by the poisoning. Once that toxicology picture became clear, the route mattered as much as the toxic agent. The prosecution case was not just that poison had killed her. It was that the poison had been placed inside a drink prepared by the person closest to her, during a morning that outwardly looked routine.

**Evidence Trail**
The evidentiary spine was straightforward and strong. According to reporting from the guilty plea and sentencing, the Crown relied on the agreed statement of facts, medical evidence establishing strychnine poisoning, and the circumstances surrounding the preparation and service of the drink.

The same reporting said Michael MacKay had texted the woman with whom he was having an affair a few days earlier, writing that a goodbye would likely come in a couple of days. Concern about the suspicious nature of Cindy's death also helped push the case toward deeper investigation rather than leaving it as an unexplained collapse.

Court reporting added that Cindy was initially unwell that morning, that Michael took two of the children to school, and that she remained home with the youngest child before he returned and prepared the drink. The drink did not need elaborate camouflage. It only had to arrive in the right hands at the right moment and pass as care.

## Courtroom Snapshot

Michael MacKay had originally been charged with first-degree murder, but in November 2023 he pleaded guilty to the lesser charge of second-degree murder in Battleford. The court imposed the mandatory life sentence, with no chance of parole for 10 years. That sentence reflected the Canadian rule that second-degree murder carries life imprisonment, with the parole ineligibility period set by the judge.

Reporting said the sentence followed a joint submission accepted by the judge, and that he was also ordered to provide a DNA sample and received a firearms prohibition. The case resolved through a guilty plea, a formal statement of facts, and a sentence that fixed the law's final view of what had happened.

## Case Takeaway

What lingers in the MacKay case is how little a poisoned drink has to do to pass as kindness. A glass mixed for someone who feels sick carries almost no friction. It does not announce itself as an event. That is what made the route so dangerous. The object was ordinary, the setting was intimate, and the harm arrived under the cover of help.

---

**The next case leaves the private household for a café in Indonesia, where one iced coffee and one meeting would ignite a national fixation.**

## CASE 17 CITATIONS

Global News, 2023-11-20, Saskatchewan man pleads guilty to killing wife with strychnine drink -- https://globalnews.ca/news/10103500/saskatchewan-man-pleads-guilty-to-killing-wife-with-strychnine-drink/

650 CKOM, 2023-11-20, MacKay sentenced to life in prison after pleading guilty in wife's poisoning death -- https://www.ckom.com/2023/11/20/mackay-sentenced-to-life-in-prison-after-pleading-guilty-in-wifes-poisoning-death/

St. Albert Gazette, 2023-11-22, Frustrated with his life, Saskatchewan man poisons wife with strychnine -- https://www.stalbertgazette.com/beyond-local/frustrated-with-his-life-saskatchewan-man-poisons-wife-with-strychnine-7866191

## CASE 18

# AN ICED COFFEE AND A CONVICTION

What began as a social meeting in a café became a national fixation, where a single drink, a crowded courtroom, and divided public opinion fused into one of the most debated cases in recent memory.

## ICED COFFEE LAUNCHED CYANIDE TRIAL

### CASE DOSSIER

| | |
|---|---|
| **Case subject:** | Jessica Kumala Wongso |
| **Location:** | Jakarta, Indonesia |
| **Key dates:** | Jan. 2016 \| Oct. 2016 \| 2024 |
| **Victim(s):** | Wayan Mirna Salihin |
| **Method:** | Cyanide-laced iced coffee |
| **Legal status:** | Convicted |
| **Current posture:** | Convicted and sentenced in 2016; released on parole in 2024 with supervision continuing until 2032 while conviction remains in place |

The meeting was supposed to look ordinary. Three women arranged to catch up at a cafe in a Jakarta shopping mall, the kind of public setting designed to lower everyone's guard. An iced coffee sat waiting on the table before the victim arrived. Nothing about the scene announced the violence that prosecutors would later say had already been set in motion. That is what gives the Jessica Wongso case its staying power. The route was not hidden in a private kitchen or a locked room. It sat in a crowded cafe, in a drink ordered in advance, inside a setting built for conversation, convenience, and routine.

At the center of the case were Jessica Wongso and Wayan Mirna Salihin, former friends whose relationship had become strained before the meeting at Cafe Olivier. By the time the case reached court, prosecutors argued that resentment and personal grievance sat behind the poisoning.

The defense disputed both the state's motive picture and the strength of the evidence. That tension shaped the case because this was not a case built around one clear confession or a simple domestic backstory. It was a public poisoning case shaped by behavior before the meeting, the timing of the drink order, and the prosecution's argument that familiarity between the women made the setting seem harmless until it was too late. Media coverage also noted that the trial drew enormous public attention in Indonesia, with extensive television coverage that turned the cafe poisoning into a national spectacle.

Mirna Salihin became unwell at the table almost immediately after the coffee was consumed, collapsed soon after, and later died. From that moment on, the case no longer belonged to the cafe as a social space. It belonged to investigators, toxicology, and a courtroom trying to decide whether cyanide had been delivered through the iced coffee. As Reuters and ABC reported at the time of conviction, prosecutors said Wongso had laced the drink with cyanide before Salihin arrived. That allegation gave the case its focal point: not just a cafe meeting, but a pre-positioned beverage waiting at the exact moment trust was supposed to begin.

**Evidence Trail**
Reporting on the Wongso case describes an evidentiary spine that combined toxic findings, surveillance footage, timeline reconstruction, and observed behavior around the table. Reporting from 2016 noted that prosecutors argued that cyanide in the coffee caused the death and that Wongso's actions before and during the meeting supported the case.

The defense attacked both the forensic certainty and the interpretation of the footage, contending that the prosecution had not proved murder beyond reasonable doubt. That dispute gave the trial unusual public intensity. The route here was visible in a public setting, but the proof still depended on how the physical evidence and the recorded movements were read. The cafe itself became part of the case record. The order, the timing, and the waiting drink all became part of the proof.

## Courtroom Snapshot

In October 2016, an Indonesian court found Jessica Wongso guilty of murdering Mirna Salihin by poisoning her iced coffee with cyanide and sentenced her to 20 years in prison. Reuters reported that the judges accepted the prosecution case, while the defense maintained that the evidence was insufficient and flawed. The verdict fixed the legal posture of the case. Years later, ABC News Australia reported that Wongso was released on parole in 2024 after serving part of the sentence, but the conviction itself remained in place.

The case is a conviction case, not an allegation case. But its public life did not end with sentencing, because release later pushed the cafe poisoning back into headlines without undoing the courtroom result.

## Case Takeaway

What marks this case is how poison moved through a setting that felt too public to be dangerous. A cafe is built for witnesses, movement, noise, and normalcy. That usually makes it feel safer than a private home. In this case, prosecutors said the public setting did not block the act. It helped disguise it. The iced coffee did not need the intimacy of a household to become lethal. It only needed trust, timing, and a person who believed a waiting drink could still be treated as hospitality. The table was out in the open. The danger, the court said, was already in the glass.

---

From a public café, the story turns back to domestic life in America, where charm, courtship, and a smiling exterior masked one of the era's most notorious female killers.

## CASE 18 CITATIONS

Reuters, 2016-10-27, Indonesian woman gets 20 years for poisoned coffee murder -- https://www.reuters.com/article/world/indonesian-woman-gets-20-years-for-poisoned-coffee-murder-idUSKCN12R18Q/

ABC News (AU), 2016-10-27, Jessica Wongso found guilty in cyanide coffee murder -- https://www.abc.net.au/news/2016-10-27/cyanide-coffee-murder-jessica-wongso-found-guilty/7971498

ABC News (AU), 2024-08-27, Convicted murderer Jessica Wongso released from prison -- https://www.abc.net.au/news/2024-08-27/convicted-murderer-jessica-wongso-released-from-prison/104260390

## CASE 19

# THE GIGGLING GRANNY

This case draws its power from contrast: the soft image of homemaking and courtship on one side, and a trail of death on the other, joined by a woman who seemed almost impossible to square with the crimes.

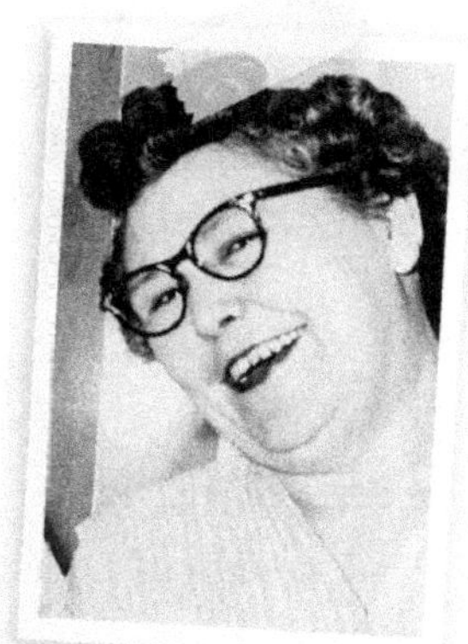

# HOME COOKING HID A KILLER

## CASE DOSSIER

| | |
|---|---|
| **Case subject:** | Nannie Doss |
| **Location:** | USA, with conviction in Oklahoma |
| **Key dates:** | 1954 \| 1955 |
| **Victim(s):** | Samuel Doss \| multiple earlier family members later linked through confessions and retrospective accounts |
| **Method:** | Arsenic-laced food and drink |
| **Legal status:** | Convicted |
| **Current posture:** | Sentenced to life imprisonment in 1955; died in prison in 1965 |

By the time Samuel Doss died in 1954, nothing on a mid-century kitchen table would have needed to look remarkable. A cup of coffee, a plate set down after a meal, a slice of pie passed across the table: those were the ordinary motions of domestic life, not scenes that invited suspicion.

That is what gives the Nannie Doss case its force. It did not turn on one spectacular serving or one instantly recognizable poisoning. It gathered weight through repetition inside ordinary household routine. When Oklahoma authorities focused on Samuel Doss's death, the pattern behind it began to stretch backward through marriages, meals, drinks, and a family history that no longer read like misfortune alone.

Nannie Doss moved through the familiar roles expected of a mid-century wife and mother. She cooked, served, kept house, and occupied the intimate routines that gave her repeated access to food and drink. That ordinary position gave her repeated access, more than any single recipe or vessel could explain. Long before the law reached Samuel Doss, deaths had accumulated around her family life.

Historical summaries and retrospective reporting link her by confession and later inquiry to several husbands and other relatives, with sources differing on the full number and identities involved. What the record supports clearly is the pattern's shape: husbands who died, family members whose deaths later drew suspicion, and a woman whose domestic place gave her repeated opportunity to administer harm without needing spectacle or force.

Samuel Doss was the husband whose death finally anchored the case in court, but the suspicion did not feel self-contained once investigators began looking behind him. The pattern carried weight because it suggested continuity: the same access, the same intimacy, the same domestic setting repeatedly turned into cover.

Samuel Doss's death in 1954 changed the scale of the case. Once his body was exhumed and arsenic was found, the question stopped being whether one husband had died unexpectedly. Investigators were then looking at a woman already surrounded by earlier losses. Reports of confession widened the frame still further. What had looked like an isolated domestic death began to read as the legal entry point into a much larger sequence.

## Evidence Trail

The legal case was strongest where it was narrowest. Toxicology fixed arsenic in Samuel Doss's remains, giving prosecutors a clear poisoning route and a specific death they could prove. From there, the public understanding of Nannie Doss widened through her reported admissions and through renewed attention to earlier family deaths. Some accounts name multiple husbands, children, a mother, a sister, and a grandchild among the suspected dead, though the exact list varies by source and was not adjudicated in one sweeping trial. That distinction needs to stay clear. The conviction rested on Samuel Doss. The broader serial pattern came from confession, investigation, and historical reconstruction layered over the formal court record.

Even without a single omnibus prosecution, that accumulation changed how the case was understood. One proved poisoning death made the older losses legible in a different way.

## Courtroom Snapshot

Nannie Doss pleaded guilty to the murder of Samuel Doss in Oklahoma in 1955 and received a life sentence. Prosecutors did not carry the wider suspected body count into a series of separate trials, in part because the Samuel Doss conviction already secured a life term. That is why the formal legal record is both firm and narrow: one principal murder conviction, one sentence, one state proceeding. The larger reputation attached to her name grew from reported confessions, subsequent inquiries, and later retellings rather than from a courtroom tally that tried every suspected death. She died in prison in 1965 from leukemia.

## Case Takeaway

One exhumed body and one arsenic finding were enough to throw years of family deaths into a harsher light. That is what makes this case endure. The cup, the meal, and the household role were not incidental details but the camouflage that let suspicion disperse for years. Familiarity can absorb doubt when deaths arrive one by one inside rituals people are least inclined to question. The law fixed only one conviction. The shadow cast by that conviction is what still lingers.

---

The next case changes scale again. What seemed like a casual neighborly gesture would soon reveal how poison could cross the boundary between households just as easily as it crossed a table.

## CASE 19 CITATIONS

Encyclopedia of Alabama, 2014-07-29, Nannie Doss -- https://encyclopediaofalabama.org/article/nannie-doss/

Wikipedia, Nannie Doss -- https://en.wikipedia.org/wiki/Nannie_Doss

## CASE 20

# BOTTLED SOFT DRINK NEXT DOOR

The menace in this story comes from how casually it arrived, disguised as a neighborly gesture while carrying poison behind the appearance of everyday generosity.

## SOFT DRINK GIFT KILLED NEXT DOOR

### CASE DOSSIER

| | |
|---|---|
| **Case subject:** | George Trepal |
| **Location:** | Alturas, Florida, USA |
| **Key dates:** | 1988 \| 1991 \| 1993 and 1997 \| 2022 |
| **Victim(s):** | Peggy Carr \| additional family members seriously poisoned |
| **Method:** | Poisoned soft-drink bottles left with neighbors |
| **Legal status:** | Convicted |
| **Current posture:** | Conviction stood; death sentence was vacated in 2022 and reduced to life |

The bottles looked like a casual gift. That is what made them dangerous. Two glass Coca-Cola bottles left at a neighbor's home belonged to the language of ordinary suburbia, the kind of small handoff that does not usually invite suspicion. In Alturas, Florida, that ordinary object became the route to one of the most chilling neighborhood poisoning cases on record.

By the time the Carr family drank from the bottles, the scene had already shifted from familiar courtesy to something much colder. The case begins there because the delivery route mattered as much as the poison itself. The bottles were not taken from a store shelf by chance. They were placed where someone expected them to be trusted.

George Trepal lived near the Carr family in a small central Florida community. The prosecution theory that later prevailed in court was not built around a domestic marriage, a family meal, or a workplace dispute. It was built around neighborhood hostility and fixation.

According to the Florida Supreme Court record, the state argued that Trepal targeted the Carr family after becoming consumed by resentment toward them and the people around them. That is what gives the case a different shape from many others. The pressure here was not household collapse. It was grievance carried outward, into the shared space between homes.

Family members became violently sick after drinking from the Coca-Cola bottles, and Peggy Carr later died. Investigators discovered that the bottles had been laced with thallium, a poison more often associated with hidden, difficult-to-trace harm than obvious attack. Once that finding entered the case, the bottles ceased to be ordinary trash or neighborhood clutter. They became the focal objects in a murder inquiry, and the street between the houses became part of the route.

## Evidence Trail

The evidence trail in the Trepal case was found by the trial court and the Florida Supreme Court to be sufficient to support capital murder and attempted-murder convictions.

The Florida Supreme Court opinions describe the state's theory in detail: poisoned Coca-Cola bottles were placed where the Carr family would find and drink them, causing mass illness and Peggy Carr's death. As described in the Florida Supreme Court opinions, the prosecution linked Trepal to thallium, to the method, and to the intent behind the placement.

The case did not depend on a single confession or one dramatic witness. It depended on the poisoned bottles, the resulting toxic injuries, and the surrounding proof that the delivery had been deliberate. That gave the case a clean and brutal structure. The route was local, personal, and designed to look harmless until it was too late.

## Courtroom Snapshot

George Trepal was convicted of first-degree murder for Peggy Carr's death and of multiple counts of attempted murder for the poisoning of other family members. The Florida Supreme Court affirmed the convictions and death sentence on direct appeal in 1993, and later rejected postconviction challenges in 1997.

Subsequent federal proceedings resulted in Trepal's death sentence being vacated and his sentence reduced to life imprisonment, while his underlying convictions remained in place. The prosecution case accepted by the courts was that Trepal intentionally poisoned the soft-drink bottles and placed them for the Carr family to consume. The later sentencing change did not erase that legal core.

## Case Takeaway

What lingers in the Trepal case is the bottle itself. A cola bottle is almost aggressively ordinary. It belongs to porches, refrigerators, and shared errands. That is what gives the case its sting. The danger was not hidden in some rare laboratory route. It was hidden in a product that looked ready to drink and perfectly safe. The street remained quiet. The bottles did the work. The poison was chemical, but the mechanism was social.

---

**From one American neighborhood, the story moves to a holiday gathering, where a Thanksgiving meal would become entangled with suspicion, toxic intent, and family trust.**

## CASE 20 CITATIONS

Justia, Florida Supreme Court, 1993, Trepal v. State --
https://law.justia.com/cases/florida/supreme-court/1993/77667-0.html

Justia, Florida Supreme Court, 1997, Trepal v. State (postconviction) --
https://law.justia.com/cases/florida/supreme-court/1997/87222-0.html

FSU Law Library, Florida Supreme Court docket PDF --
https://library.law.fsu.edu/Digital-
Collections/flsupct/dockets/94505/94505b.pdf

132

## CASE 21

# THE THANKSGIVING DINNER

Thanksgiving is built around trust, closeness, and the idea of home, which makes this case all the more jarring when investigators began tracing a death back to something consumed during the dinner.

## THANKSGIVING TABLE HID DEADLY PLAN

### CASE DOSSIER

| | |
|---|---|
| **Case subject:** | Gudrun Linda Casper-Leinenkugel |
| **Location:** | Henderson County, North Carolina, USA |
| **Key dates:** | Nov. 27, 2025 \| Jan. 2026 \| Feb. 2026 |
| **Victim(s):** | Leela Jean Livis \| Mia Lacey (survived) Richard Pegg (survived) \| Michael Schmidt also alleged in earlier death |
| **Method:** | Acetonitrile allegedly administered in Thanksgiving meal or drinks |
| **Legal status:** | Indicted |
| **Current posture:** | Held without bond in 2026 on murder and attempted murder charges |

The Thanksgiving table should have been the safest place in the house. Plates were passed, glasses were filled, and the evening followed the familiar rhythm of a family meal. Then prosecutors alleged that one bottle of wine had carried something far more dangerous than alcohol. What followed was not instant public chaos but confusion, illness, hospital treatment, and the slow collapse of confidence around an ordinary family ritual. The power of the case comes from that setting. A Thanksgiving table depends on repetition, trust, and the assumption that what is shared is safe. Prosecutors say that trust is what made the alleged poisoning possible.

At the center of the case is Gudrun Linda Casper-Leinenkugel, charged in North Carolina with murder and attempted murder counts arising from the 2025 Thanksgiving gathering. Reporting on the warrants said the dinner brought together family members, including her daughters and one daughter's boyfriend. That made the alleged route of harm especially intimate. This was not a stranger contamination case and not a random public-health scare. It was an allegation that danger moved through a family table, by way of a bottle poured among people who had reason to trust the setting and each other.

The pressure on the case deepened when investigators also tied Casper-Leinenkugel to the 2007 death of Michael Schmidt. That older allegation changed the scale of the prosecution theory. The state was no longer describing a single night of suspected poisoning. Prosecutors were describing what they say is a pattern stretching across nearly two decades.

Investigators moved the case into a homicide posture after the illness stopped looking unexplained and the wine itself became central to the allegations. According to warrant coverage, authorities believe acetonitrile was added to the bottle served during the Thanksgiving dinner. From there, the case widened sharply. Prosecutors later alleged that the 2025 poisoning was not the beginning of the story but part of a longer arc that also reached back to Michael Schmidt's 2007 death. Once that allegation entered the record, the case no longer turned only on one holiday gathering. It became a prosecution theory built on two alleged poisonings separated by eighteen years.

## Evidence Trail

Because the case is still active, the evidence has to be described as the state's allegation rather than settled fact. Reporting on the warrants said investigators believe acetonitrile was added to wine served to Leela Livis, Mia Lacey, and Richard Pegg during the Thanksgiving gathering. Prosecutors further alleged that Livis died and the other two suffered serious injury.

Local coverage also reported that the dinner involved about a dozen people, but that the charging theory focused on a particular bottle and particular glasses rather than on the entire meal becoming dangerous. That specificity narrows the state's theory. The state's case, as reported so far, depends on what was poured, who received it, and what investigators say the chemical would do once metabolized in the body.

The case widened further when authorities charged Casper-Leinenkugel in connection with Schmidt's 2007 death. That older allegation is one of the most striking features of the case because it turns a single holiday poisoning prosecution into something broader and more unsettling. At this stage there has been no trial, no tested defense case, and no jury verdict. What exists is the charging record, the warrant theory, and the prosecution's claim that the same defendant stands at the center of both alleged poisonings.

**Courtroom Snapshot**

As of late February 2026, reporting said a grand jury had indicted Casper-Leinenkugel on two counts of first-degree murder, two counts of attempted first-degree murder, and multiple counts tied to distributing a prohibited food or beverage containing a toxic chemical. Early reporting suggested the state might seek the death penalty, and a Rule 24 filing briefly pointed in that direction, but prosecutors later announced they would not pursue capital punishment. A probable-cause hearing was canceled after the indictment, and she remained jailed without bond.

The most important legal fact is the simplest one: this case has not been tried. The indictment means prosecutors persuaded a grand jury that the charges should proceed, not that guilt has been proved. All counts remain allegations, and Casper-Leinenkugel is presumed innocent unless and until proven guilty in court. No trial date had been set in the cited reporting, so the public record still shows a charged case waiting to be tested rather than a completed prosecution.

**Case Takeaway**

Thanksgiving should have been a ritual of repetition, comfort, and family memory. Prosecutors instead say it became the setting for poison delivered through shared wine. What makes the case especially difficult to look away from is that it does not end with one night. The charging theory reaches backward to an older death and asks the court to treat the 2025 allegations as part of a longer pattern.

That is the shape of the case. It is not only about a holiday meal. It is about whether two alleged poisonings, eighteen years apart, can be understood as part of the same history. Because there has been no trial, the case closes not with a verdict but with an unresolved record: the bottle opened, the charges filed, the older death brought forward again, and the final judgment still ahead.

---

**The next case steps back into nineteenth-century France, where arsenic, marriage, and courtroom spectacle combined to create a poisoning story that has never fully settled.**

## CASE 21 CITATIONS

ABC11 (WTVD), 2026-02-26, NC woman accused of poisoning family on Thanksgiving could face death penalty -- https://abc11.com/post/nc-woman-accused-poisoning-family-thanksgiving-could-face-death-penalty/18653015/

Court TV, 2026-02-28, Prosecutors: No death penalty for mom accused of poisoning Thanksgiving dinner -- https://www.courttv.com/news/prosecutors-no-death-penalty-for-mom-accused-of-poisoning-thanksgiving-dinner/

WLOS, 2026-01-28, Warrants say woman poisoned family at Thanksgiving -- https://wlos.com/news/local/henderson-county-arrest-warrants-district-court-gundrun-linda-jean-casper-leinenkugel-first-degree-murder-attempted-multiple-counts-prohibited-food-beverage-toxic-chemical-serious-physical-injury-death-thanksgiving-patton-public-house

## CASE 22

# CAKE, CHEMISTRY, CONVICTION

This case moves beyond a simple poisoning allegation into the realm of obsession, reputation, and doubt, where arsenic, marriage, and courtroom drama became impossible to separate.

## CAKE AND ARSENIC SHOOK FRANCE.

### CASE DOSSIER

| | |
|---|---|
| **Case subject:** | Marie Lafarge |
| **Location:** | Le Glandier near Objat, Corrèze, France |
| **Key dates:** | Jan. 1840 \| 1840 |
| **Victim(s):** | Charles Lafarge |
| **Method:** | Arsenic poisoning, allegedly administered through food and drink |
| **Legal status:** | Convicted |
| **Current posture:** | Sentenced to life at hard labor; later commuted, released early on health |

The marriage had already soured by the time the illness began. At Le Glandier in the winter of 1840, Charles Lafarge grew sick, recovered briefly, then worsened again. The household around him shifted from care to suspicion.

Later retellings would fasten on the cake, because it gives the story an object a reader can hold in the mind: domestic, ordinary, sent from one room into another. But the real force of the case was larger than a single baked item. Once Charles died, the question was not only whether poison had moved through a household meal. It was whether a criminal court could be persuaded by chemistry.

Marie Capelle had married into the Lafarge name expecting security and status, and found instead a disappointing estate, mounting strain, and a husband she did not admire. Prosecutors used that unhappy marriage as the emotional logic of the case. They argued that resentment, money pressure, and disillusionment gave the poisoning its motive.

The defense pushed back, portraying Marie not as a calculating poisoner but as a woman trapped inside a bad match and a public scandal. That tension matters because this was never just a science case. It was also a marriage case, with every forensic claim filtered through questions about intimacy, expectation, and distrust. Charles's sickness stopped looking like an unfortunate domestic illness once sustained suspicion of arsenic took hold. From there, the case widened quickly.

Prosecutors argued that poison had been administered through food and drink over time, and the cake Marie allegedly sent became one of the best-known features of the prosecution story, even though it was not the only alleged route discussed.

Once arsenic entered the frame, the case no longer belonged only to the household. It belonged to experts, laboratories, and a courtroom trying to decide how much certainty science could honestly supply.

## Evidence Trail

The prosecution built its case from a combination of symptoms, surrounding circumstances, arsenic purchases, and toxicological testing.

Accounts of the trial note that Marie bought arsenic several times in the weeks before Charles Lafarge's death, purchases the prosecution treated as highly significant. But what made the trial historically important was the battle over proof.

Chemists and physicians were drawn into the proceedings, and the work associated with Mathieu Orfila and early arsenic detection methods became central to the public understanding of the case.

The issue was not merely whether arsenic could be suspected. It was whether it could be demonstrated in a way strong enough to support a conviction.

The prosecution said the symptoms, testing, and surrounding evidence pointed to deliberate poisoning. The defense attacked the reliability of the analysis and argued that the science was being asked to carry more certainty than it truly could. That argument outlived the verdict.

The Lafarge case became one of the nineteenth century's defining examples of toxicology moving from specialist knowledge into the heart of criminal law.

## Courtroom Snapshot

Marie Lafarge was tried in 1840 for poisoning her husband, Charles, with arsenic. The court accepted the prosecution case and convicted her, sentencing her to life at hard labor. The sentence was later commuted, and she was eventually released early because of ill health. Legally, the case ends as a conviction.

Historically, it remained unsettled in another sense. Later generations kept returning to it because the verdict seemed to rest not only on motive and suspicion, but on a form of scientific proof that still felt new enough to be contested in public. That is why the trial remained famous long after the marriage itself had vanished into history.

## Case Takeaway

The alleged cake route gives the case its domestic shape. The chemistry gives it its lasting importance. A failing marriage could explain why suspicion formed. It could not, by itself, justify conviction.

What gave the case such endurance was the courtroom struggle over whether toxicology could convert suspicion into proof. In some poisoning prosecutions, the most decisive witness is not the spouse, the servant, or the doctor, but the laboratory.

---

**From historical France, the story returns to modern America, where the target was not a spouse but a child, and the poison was delivered in the most vulnerable setting imaginable.**

## CASE 22 CITATIONS

Encyclopaedia Britannica, Marie Lafarge -- https://www.britannica.com/biography/Marie-Lafarge

Legal-historical summaries of the Lafarge poisoning case and the toxicology evidence associated with Mathieu Orfila and early arsenic testing

## CASE 23

# ANTIFREEZE IN THE NURSERY

There are few allegations more disturbing than one that reaches into a nursery, and this case remains so haunting because it placed poison where protection should have been absolute.

## BABY BOTTLE HELD ANTIFREEZE

### CASE DOSSIER

| | |
|---|---|
| **Case subject:** | Curtis Jack |
| **Location:** | Fulton County, Georgia, USA |
| **Key dates:** | 2023 \| Apr. 2024 |
| **Victim(s):** | Newborn daughter |
| **Method:** | Antifreeze in infant bottle |
| **Legal status:** | Convicted |
| **Current posture:** | Sentenced in 2024 to 50 years in prison |

A newborn cannot choose what enters her bottle. It belongs to feeding, nourishment, and the small repeated acts that keep a newborn alive through the night.

That is what makes this case so hard to read and so impossible to forget. In Georgia, prosecutors said the route of harm was not hidden in a stranger's package or a contaminated product line. It was in the bottles meant for an infant. Once doctors, hospital staff, and investigators understood what had entered the child's system, the object at the center of the case changed completely. It was no longer part of ordinary care. It was evidence.

Curtis Jack was the child's father, which gives the case its emotional structure immediately. This is not a case built around a social drink, a workplace lunch, or a contested inheritance. It is a caretaker case. The state's theory, as reflected in the sentencing reporting from 2024, was that the person with direct access to the newborn's feeding bottles used that access to introduce antifreeze. That places the case in a more vulnerable register than many others. The delivery route depended on dependency itself.

The case hardened when the infant became critically ill and medical testing no longer supported an innocent explanation. Reporting said the child tested positive for ethylene glycol, the toxic chemical found in antifreeze. Hospital staff alerted authorities when the baby's condition and toxicology results raised suspicion, prompting an investigation that focused on what she had been fed at home.

Once that finding entered the record, the investigation narrowed around how the poison had been delivered and who had controlled the feeding route.

The bottle became the case's focal object. There was no need for elaborate staging. The state's claim was stark on its own: poison had been placed where nourishment was supposed to be.

## Evidence Trail

The evidentiary spine was built around toxicology, access, and the condition of the child after feeding. KATV and People both reported that the newborn survived but suffered catastrophic injuries after ethylene glycol was found in her system. According to the sentencing coverage, prosecutors relied on the positive toxicology, the feeding-bottle route, and additional evidence linking Curtis Jack to the act, rather than on a broader pattern of prior incidents. That compact structure gives the case its shape. It is a single-route poisoning case, but one where the route carried an unusual moral weight because the victim was entirely dependent on whoever prepared the bottle.

## Courtroom Snapshot

Curtis Jack was sentenced in April 2024 after the Georgia case concluded with a severe prison term. Reporting said he received 50 years for poisoning his newborn daughter with antifreeze placed in baby bottles. The prosecution case treated the act as deliberate and devastating, with the surviving child left permanently harmed. The defense did not prevent the final sentencing outcome reported in the case coverage. The legal posture is clear: a completed conviction with a fixed sentence, not an allegation file or a historic mystery.

**Case Takeaway**

This case turns on the feeding route. The poison did not travel through a drink shared among adults or a meal set on a family table. According to prosecutors, it moved through bottles prepared for a newborn who could only take what a caregiver placed in front of her. That fact gives the evidence its lasting weight. The object at the center is small, ordinary, and inseparable from care, which is why the poisoning reads less like a hidden trick than a breach of dependency itself.

---

**The next case shifts back to Britain, where a home-cooked curry became the center of a case that helped shape one woman's dark and lasting reputation.**


## CASE 23 CITATIONS

KATV, 2024-04-14, Man sentenced after poisoning newborn daughter with antifreeze -- https://katv.com/news/nation-world/man-poisoned-newborn-daughter-antifreeze-sentenced-50-years-prison-curtis-jack-fulton-county-georgia-poisoning-breast-milk-hospitalized-child-critically-ill-injuries-test-positive-ethylene-glycol-investigation-police-detectives-custody

People, 2024-04-14, Man who tried to kill baby with antifreeze sentenced to 50 years -- https://people.com/man-who-tried-to-kill-baby-with-antifreeze-sentenced-to-50-years-8631184

# THE BLACK WIDOW'S CURRY

**By the time this meal took on its full meaning, the story had already become one of betrayal, calculation, and a reputation dark enough to outlive the trial itself.**

## CURRY DINNER ENDED IN BETRAYAL

---

### CASE DOSSIER

| | |
|---|---|
| **Case subject:** | Dena Thompson |
| **Location:** | Sussex, England, UK |
| **Key dates:** | 1992 \| 1996 \| 2003 |
| **Victim(s):** | Julian Webb \| Richard Thompson (survived) |
| **Method:** | Antidepressant-laced curry |
| **Legal status:** | Convicted |
| **Current posture:** | Convicted in 2003 of murder and attempted murder; life sentence imposed |

---

Curry is the kind of home dinner that can disappear into routine, served hot, eaten quickly, and cleared without ceremony.

In this case, that familiarity became part of the prosecution theory. The question was not whether a stranger had brought something suspicious to the door. It was whether an ordinary domestic meal had been used to poison two men close to the same woman, years apart. That is what gives the case its grip. The food at the center was common. The pattern around it was not.

Dena Thompson later became widely known in British reporting as the "Black Widow", a nickname that reflects the case's pattern but also risks flattening it into tabloid shorthand. A cleaner way to read the case is this: two men close to her were poisoned in separate episodes, and prosecutors argued that money sat behind both attacks. Julian Webb, Thompson's former partner, survived. Peter Thompson, her husband, died. What linked the episodes was not theatrical violence but access, trust, and a domestic setting in which a served meal did not immediately look like a criminal act.

Investigators eventually stopped treating the two episodes as isolated illnesses and began reading them as a connected pattern. Julian Webb had survived poisoning in 1992. Years later, after Peter Thompson died in 1996, police pulled those threads together. The prosecution said both men had been given curry containing large doses of antidepressants and other drugs, in lethal or near-lethal quantities. Once that pattern became central to the Crown's case, the matter was no longer about one suspicious death. It became about repetition and whether the later meal cast light backward onto the earlier one.

## Evidence Trail

The evidentiary strength of the case came from its pattern. Prosecutors argued that Thompson had poisoned Julian Webb in 1992 in an attempt to kill him, then used the same basic method against Peter Thompson in 1996. Reporting on the trial said the Crown linked the acts through motive, timing, and toxic findings, with financial gain presented as a central reason throughout.

Reporting emphasized that the prosecution case relied on the jury accepting that two separate domestic poisonings were connected and intentional, rather than on a single dramatic confession or a lone forensic breakthrough.

## Courtroom Snapshot

In 2003, Dena Thompson was convicted of murdering her husband Peter Thompson, who died in 1996, and attempting to murder her former partner Julian Webb, who survived poisoning in 1992. Reporting from the time said the prosecution persuaded the jury that she had used curry laced with large doses of antidepressants and other drugs to poison both men in separate episodes.

She was sentenced to life imprisonment, with a recommended minimum term reported as 16 years. She was also convicted on fraud-related counts. That result turns what could have looked like two isolated domestic tragedies into one legally established pattern. The court accepted repetition as evidence of design.

## Case Takeaway

The poison route in this case is almost aggressively ordinary. Curry is not a ceremonial dish or a rare delicacy. It is just dinner. That is what lets the pattern do so much work. One meal might be dismissed. Two linked poisonings force a different reading. The more routine the serving looks, the more power a repeated pattern can carry once investigators connect it. Domestic familiarity did not hide the case forever. It made the final pattern more damning.

---

**From a private meal, the story moves into the social ritual of celebration, where a champagne toast would become unforgettable for all the wrong reasons.**

## CASE 24 CITATIONS

The Guardian, 2003, coverage of Dena Thompson's conviction and life sentence -- https://www.theguardian.com/uk/2003/aug/28/ukcrime

Independent, archive coverage of the Black Widow poisoning case -- https://www.independent.co.uk/

Murderpedia summary for chronology cross-checking -- https://murderpedia.org/female.T/t/thompson-dena.htm

## CASE 25

# CHAMPAGNE TOAST

A toast is supposed to seal a joyful moment. Here, it became the detail that made the case unforgettable, because what followed shattered the occasion with terrifying speed.

## CHAMPAGNE TOAST CARRIED CYANIDE

### CASE DOSSIER

| | |
|---|---|
| **Case subject:** | Harlow Fraden and Dennis Wepman |
| **Location:** | Bronx/Manhattan, New York City, USA |
| **Key dates:** | Aug. 1953 \| Dec. 1953 |
| **Victim(s):** | Dr. William Fraden and Shirley Fraden |
| **Method:** | Cyanide in champagne |
| **Legal status:** | Convicted |
| **Current posture:** | Fraden declared criminally insane and committed to Matteawan State Hospital; died in 1960. Wepman found sane and sentenced to 20 years to life; paroled 1968 |

A champagne toast belongs to the grammar of celebration. It signals arrival, relief, success, the brief pause before people return to talking and music. That is what makes this case so disturbing. In August 1953, the drink did not simply accompany the crime.

It was the method. Harlow Fraden, a chemistry graduate, mixed potassium cyanide into two glasses of champagne in his parents' kitchen, carried them back to the living room, announced a new job, and raised a toast. His parents drank and collapsed. What happened next turned a domestic ritual into a double killing.

Contemporaneous reporting named Harlow Fraden as the son who poisoned his parents and Dennis Wepman, his roommate, as the friend drawn into the plot. The victims were William Fraden, a physician, and Shirley Fraden, a schoolteacher.

The pressure in the case came from resentment, dependence, money, and grievance. TIME portrayed Fraden as a chemistry graduate locked in bitter conflict with his parents, especially his mother, while still financially reliant on them. According to that reporting, once his allowance was cut, Fraden concluded that life would be easier if his parents were gone. Wepman entered the story not as a stranger at the edge of events but as someone with advance knowledge of the plan. Chemistry World later reported that Wepman took notes in the corridor while the attack was carried out inside the apartment.

What makes the case linger is the way the murder method borrowed the shape of celebration. Fraden reportedly arrived with champagne, announced good news about a new job, and turned the family ritual of a toast into a killing mechanism. The drink was not incidental. It was the method.

The deaths were initially recorded as a suicide pact and remained unsolved for four months. The case shifted only after Fraden and Wepman fell out. At a party in December 1953, Wepman confided in a woman he knew, who went to the police. Wepman then gave a full account. Fraden initially refused to speak but eventually talked after police accused him of killing for financial gain. Both men were arrested and murder charges followed.

Once those accounts were on the record, the scene in the parents' apartment changed completely. The champagne toast was no longer a staged suicide. It was a planned homicide carried out through a familiar social script, with poison mixed in the kitchen before the glasses were brought to the table.

## Evidence Trail

The evidentiary spine ran through reported confessions, physical evidence at the scene, and the reconstruction of a deliberately staged suicide. According to contemporaneous newspaper coverage, Fraden had tested a mixture of champagne and potassium cyanide before the killings to see whether the poison would be visible. Chemistry World reported that bitters were also added to the glasses to conceal any change in the champagne's color.

After the killings, Fraden and Wepman disposed of the third glass, which Fraden had kept clean for himself, to remove evidence of the three-glass arrangement, then returned two days later to discover the bodies and report them to police.

That structure gave the case unusual clarity in retrospect. It did not depend on a single dramatic witness or a chance forensic find. The method survived in the record through the perpetrators' own accounts, the physical evidence at the scene, and the deliberate staging the pair attempted afterward. Once both men had spoken, the route was documented in detail: champagne, potassium cyanide, bitters, kitchen preparation, living room delivery, and a false toast.

## Courtroom Snapshot

Harlow Fraden was declared criminally insane by Bellevue Hospital psychiatrists and committed to Matteawan State Hospital for the Criminally Insane in February 1954. He died there in 1960. Dennis Wepman was found sane and sentenced to 20 years to life. He was taken to Sing Sing and later paroled in 1968.

The two outcomes reflect the different legal paths the case took from a shared arrest. Fraden never faced a conventional trial. Wepman did, and the sentence was substantial. Together they fix the case in the formal record: not a mystery, not an unsolved poisoning, but a double murder carried out through a champagne toast, with one perpetrator institutionalized and the other imprisoned.

**Case Takeaway**

The delivery route in this case does not hide inside care, marriage, or family duty. It hides inside celebration. Champagne carries built-in symbolism. It marks a high point. Here, that symbolism became camouflage. The drink that should have stood for pleasure and status instead appears in the record as a measured delivery system. The method worked because the setting asked the victims to lower their guard.

Poison does not always arrive disguised as medicine, food, or concern. Sometimes it arrives dressed as good news, already poured, already raised, already halfway to the lips.

---

**The next case brings the danger back inside the home, where shared drinks, a staged note, and shifting suspicion made the truth far harder to pin down.**

**CASE 25 CITATIONS**

TIME, 1953-12-28, CRIME: Champagne and Cyanide --
https://time.com/archive/6795850/crime-champagne-cyanide/

Chemistry World, 2024-12-17, The champagne cases --
https://www.chemistryworld.com/opinion/the-champagne-cases/4020552.article

Trove, 1953-12-19, Cyanide killer may have killed others --
https://trove.nla.gov.au/newspaper/article/47562736

## CASE 26

# DRINKS AT HOME

What should have remained a private domestic evening instead unraveled into a case of poison, staged evidence, and suspicion that shifted in ways almost as disturbing as the death itself.

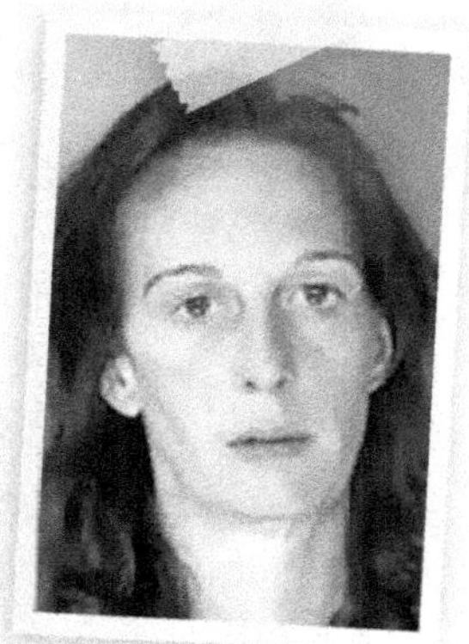

## DRINKS AT HOME TURNED LETHAL

---

**CASE DOSSIER**

| | |
|---|---|
| **Case subject:** | Stacey Castor |
| **Location:** | Onondaga County, New York, USA |
| **Key dates:** | 2000 \| 2005 \| 2007 \| 2009 |
| **Victim(s):** | David Castor \| Ashley Wallace (survived) Michael Wallace linked in earlier death |
| **Method:** | Antifreeze-poisoned drinks |
| **Legal status:** | Convicted |
| **Current posture:** | Convicted in 2009 and sentenced to 51 2/3 years to life; died in prison in 2016 |

The note was supposed to close the story before anyone asked harder questions.

Typed as a confession and left to point blame elsewhere, it gave prosecutors a way to argue that this case was never only about what had been poured into a glass. A drink inside the house could be made to look ordinary. A note left in the same house could be made to look final. In the Stacey Castor case, prosecutors said both were used together: poison to harm, paper to redirect suspicion.

Stacey Castor's name became nationally known because prosecutors argued she had already moved through one suspicious husband's death before another followed. Her first husband, Michael Wallace, died in 2000. Her second husband, David Castor, died in 2005. Investigators later revisited the earlier death while building the case around the second. What tightened the pressure, though, was not only the marital pattern. It was the state's claim that Castor tried to kill her daughter Ashley Wallace and leave behind a false confession note so the family story would close in the wrong direction.

After David Castor's death, investigators began treating the scene as something more deliberate than suicide or unexplained poisoning. Prosecutors said antifreeze had been administered through a drink, and they argued that Stacey Castor then tried to strengthen the appearance of suicide by arranging evidence and planting a typed note. The case widened again when Ashley Wallace was later given a drugged drink and survived, an episode prosecutors used to present the matter as a deliberate pattern rather than a single suspicious death.

## Evidence Trail

The evidentiary spine was stronger than a single toxic finding. The state's case rested on the antifreeze death of David Castor, the later attempted poisoning of Ashley Wallace, and the manufactured note prosecutors said was designed to place responsibility on the daughter. ABC's timeline reporting describes how those pieces fit together: one husband dead, another earlier death reconsidered, a daughter nearly killed, and a prosecution arguing that the defendant's effort to script the aftermath was itself part of the crime. That is important because the case is not only about what was served. It is also about what was written after the fact, and how the attempt to control the story became additional evidence.

## Courtroom Snapshot

In 2009, Stacey Castor was convicted of second-degree murder for David Castor's death, attempted second-degree murder for the poisoning of Ashley Wallace, and forgery for the fake suicide note. Prosecutors said she poisoned her husband, then tried to poison her daughter and frame her for the death with a fabricated confession. The defense challenged the state's interpretation, but the jury accepted the broader pattern. She was sentenced to 51 and two-thirds years to life in prison, effectively a life term, and died behind bars in 2016. The legal posture is firm: a conviction for one completed murder, one attempted murder, and a staged paper trail the jury treated as part of the same scheme.

**Case Takeaway**

The note is what gives this case its lasting shape. The poisoned drink sat at the center of the case, and so did the setting: home, marriage, familiarity. But the feature that set this prosecution apart was the effort to script the aftermath. Prosecutors said the false confession was not an afterthought but part of the same scheme, an attempt to write blame onto someone who survived. The jury accepted that argument. That is what separates this case from other domestic poisoning prosecutions: not only what was served, but the attempt to control who would be believed.

---

**From New York, the focus returns to one of Britain's most debated poisoning cases, where a late-night drink became the focal point of a controversy that never fully faded.**

**CASE 26 CITATIONS**

ABC News, 2019-02-06, Timeline: Black widow Stacey Castor's shocking crimes -- https://abcnews.go.com/US/timeline-black-widow-stacey-castors-shocking-crimes/story?id=60860538

## CASE 27

# LATE-NIGHT COCOA

Few cases linger so heavily in public memory, where one drink, one death, and one disputed account turned a private moment into an enduring criminal controversy.

## MIDNIGHT COCOA TURNED DEADLY

### CASE DOSSIER

| | |
|---|---|
| **Case subject:** | Madeleine Smith |
| **Location:** | Glasgow, Scotland, UK |
| **Key dates:** | Mar. 23, 1857 \| June-July 1857 |
| **Victim(s):** | Pierre Emile L'Angelier |
| **Method:** | Alleged arsenic-laced cocoa |
| **Legal status:** | Tried, not convicted |
| **Current posture:** | Acquitted by a verdict of not proven |

The cup belonged to the hour when the house was supposed to quiet down. A cocoa before bed suggested warmth, privacy, and routine, the sort of drink that invited trust rather than caution.

In Glasgow in 1857, that familiar domestic setting became inseparable from one of the century's most enduring poisoning cases. Pierre Emile L'Angelier fell violently ill and died after a pattern of sickness that no longer looked accidental. What followed was not a case built around a public attack or a dramatic struggle in the street. It grew out of letters, secrecy, arsenic, and a relationship that had become dangerous long before it reached a courtroom.

Madeleine Smith was a young woman from a respectable Glasgow family. L'Angelier was her lover, and the relationship existed inside a world where secrecy mattered as much as feeling. When she became engaged to another man, that earlier attachment stopped being merely compromising and started to look threatening. Victorian respectability gave the case much of its pressure.

Prosecutors argued that private correspondence, emotional entanglement, and the risk of exposure created a motive shaped by reputation, marriage prospects, and social ruin. That is what still gives the case its hold. It was never only about arsenic. It was also about what could happen when intimacy collided with status, fear, and the possibility that a hidden relationship might become public.

L'Angelier's repeated bouts of illness in February and March 1857 pushed suspicion out of the private sphere and into open inquiry. He suffered at least two serious attacks before the fatal illness on March 23, and investigators increasingly treated arsenic as the likely explanation. Attention then moved toward Madeleine Smith.

The prosecution said poison had been obtained and administered through food or drink; cocoa was one of several possible routes discussed at the time and later became the most remembered vehicle in retellings of the case. By the time the trial opened, the shape of the prosecution case was fixed: secret letters, poison purchases, a dead lover, and a defendant whose social position made every detail legible through scandal as well as law.

## Evidence Trail

Historical accounts describe the evidence against Smith as powerful in parts but incomplete as a whole. Prosecutors relied on the correspondence between Smith and L'Angelier, evidence that arsenic had been obtained, and medical testimony about the cause of death. Later summaries commonly note that Smith bought arsenic three times in the weeks before L'Angelier died, with purchases usually dated to February 12, February 19, and March 18, 1857.

The Crown argued that the relationship had become a threat and that poison offered a way out. But nineteenth-century forensic proof did not erase uncertainty in the way modern toxicology might.

Questions remained over how conclusively arsenic could be tied to one administered drink and whether the chain from purchase to delivery was complete enough to satisfy a murder charge. That tension explains why the case has endured. To many observers, then and later, the evidence looked grave, but not grave enough to force certainty.

## Courtroom Snapshot

Madeleine Smith was tried in Edinburgh in 1857 for the murder of L'Angelier. The prosecution said she had poisoned him with arsenic after the relationship became dangerous to her future. The defense attacked the gaps in proof and the distance between suspicion and certainty.

The jury returned the distinctive Scottish verdict of not proven. That outcome acquitted Smith without affirmatively declaring her factually innocent, and under Scots law it barred any retrial on the same charge. There was no murder conviction, but there was no clean exoneration either. The record has remained strong enough to sustain lasting suspicion in popular and legal history, yet uncertain enough to have prevented a guilty verdict.

## Case Takeaway

The Madeleine Smith case endures because an ingestion case can remain powerful even when the law refuses final closure. The remembered cocoa, whether treated as a literal route or as shorthand for the intimate setting of the alleged poisoning, keeps the case anchored in private evening ritual.

That is why it lingers. A secret relationship, a domestic drink, and a public trial ended not with certainty, but with a verdict designed to hold doubt in place. The unresolved quality is not incidental. It is the reason the case still feels alive.

---

**The next case changes the method but not the cruelty, following a plot built around a poisoned bottle sent under the cover of sophistication and deceit.**

## CASE 27 CITATIONS

Encyclopaedia Britannica, Madeleine Smith -- https://www.britannica.com/biography/Madeleine-Smith

Historic UK, The Madeleine Smith Case -- https://www.historic-uk.com/HistoryUK/HistoryofScotland/The-Madeleine-Smith-Case/

The National Library of Scotland, historic newspaper archive references to the 1857 trial -- https://www.nls.uk/

# JAMES HAMPSTEAD

## CASE 28

# THE FAKE WINE CLUB

Part of what gives this case its sting is the performance behind it, a false air of sophistication concealing a vindictive plot built around poison delivered by post.

**FAKE WINE CLUB HID POISON PLOT**

### CASE DOSSIER

| | |
|---|---|
| **Case subject:** | Thomas Kwan |
| **Location:** | Newcastle / Sunderland, England, UK |
| **Key dates:** | Sept. 2022-Jan. 2024 \| Nov. 2024 Oct. 2025 \| Jan. 30, 2026 |
| **Victim(s):** | Patrick O'Hara \| Torquil Gundlach also affected in wine scheme |
| **Method:** | Poisoned wine sent through a fake wine club scheme |
| **Legal status:** | Guilty plea / convicted in related plot |
| **Current posture:** | Already serving life with a 31-year minimum in separate fake-vaccine attack; pleaded guilty in 2025 in the wine plot, with sentencing listed 2026 at draft date |

The package was designed to flatter before it harmed. A bottle of wine arriving through a tasting club looks like status, courtesy, or harmless promotion. That is what made the scheme so effective in concept and so chilling in retrospect. Prosecutors said the delivery did not come from a real club at all. It came from a fake one created to make poisoned bottles look legitimate. By the time the wine reached Patrick O'Hara, the route had already borrowed the language of luxury in order to hide the intent behind it.

Thomas Kwan was already serving time for one poisoning attempt against Patrick O'Hara when the wine plot came to light. AP reported in 2024 that he had tried to kill his mother's partner by disguising himself as an NHS nurse and administering a fake COVID booster laced with poison. The later wine plot widened that case rather than replacing it.

ITV reported that between September 2022 and January 2024 Kwan had created the fictitious Northern Wine and Drinks Tasting Gentlemen's Club and sent O'Hara a mixture of genuine and poisoned bottles. The pressure in the case comes from repetition. This was not one desperate act. It was a sustained effort to remove the same man from the inheritance picture.

The wine deliveries became significant once prosecutors treated them not as clutter or promotion, but as a deliberate delivery system. ITV reported that some of the bottles were genuine and some were allegedly laced with thallium, all sent under the cover of a fake wine society.

That shift matters because the packaging was part of the method. The scheme depended on the bottles looking like something a person might keep opening.

What changed the legal picture was not one suspicious parcel on its own. It was the repeated arrival of bottles, the invented club behind them, and the alleged poisoning of more than one person linked to the scheme.

The case moved from odd luxury gifting into an attempted-murder prosecution once investigators and prosecutors treated the fake brand identity as camouflage rather than decoration.

## Evidence Trail

The evidentiary spine combined the bottles, the toxic findings, and the continuity between the wine scheme and Kwan's broader poisoning conduct. ITV reported that between 18 and 21 bottles were sent, some contaminated and some not, and that recovered bottles showed poison while a further bottle was believed to have caused illness.

The court also heard that Torquil Gundlach became unwell after being given one of the wines. That widened the harm beyond the intended primary target. The level of design is what makes the case unusual.

This was not simply poison in a bottle. It was poison hidden inside a fake brand identity, supported by genuine-looking deliveries meant to lure the recipient into confidence.

## Courtroom Snapshot

The legal posture has two parts. First, Kwan is already serving a life sentence with a minimum term of 31 years after pleading guilty in 2024 to the attempted murder of Patrick O'Hara through the fake vaccine attack, according to AP. Second, ITV reported that in October 2025 he pleaded guilty to a further attempt to murder O'Hara by sending poisoned wine and to administering a noxious substance in relation to Gundlach.

As of the time of writing, sentencing on those wine-related charges was listed for January 30, 2026. The wine case is not speculative and not merely alleged. The guilty plea fixes the route and intent more firmly than an open charge would, even though final sentencing on this part of the case was still pending.

## Case Takeaway

What lingers in this case is the fake club itself. The invented society was not a flourish around the crime. It was the crime's delivery architecture, giving poisoned bottles the look of status, routine, and legitimacy before they were opened. Trust did not sit only in the bottle. It sat in the branding, the repeated deliveries, and the fiction that a victim was receiving membership perks rather than a weapon. The label did part of the work before the liquid ever reached the glass.

---

From one calculated delivery, the story turns to colonial Australia, where poisoning, money, and a pattern of deaths made each new loss harder to explain away.

## CASE 28 CITATIONS

AP News, 2024-11-06, UK doctor gets 31 years for poisoning mother's partner with fake COVID vaccine -- https://apnews.com/article/ffc3a2fbdf8c27a561cf6d39e0525611

ITV News Tyne Tees, 2025-10-09, Former GP Dr Thomas Kwan admits further murder plot using fake wine -- https://www.itv.com/news/tyne-tees/2025-10-09/former-gp-admits-further-murder-plot-using-fake-wine

## CASE 29

# POISON, PAYOUTS, AND PROSECUTION

At the center of this case is not just arsenic, but motive, money, and a succession of deaths that made coincidence harder and harder to believe.

## DEATHS BROUGHT PAYOUTS AND SUSPICION

---

### CASE DOSSIER

| | |
|---|---|
| **Case subject:** | Martha Needle |
| **Location:** | Victoria, Australia |
| **Key dates:** | Early 1890s \| 1894 |
| **Victim(s):** | Multiple family members across a broader poisoning pattern |
| **Method:** | Arsenic poisoning in household meals and drinks |
| **Legal status:** | Convicted |
| **Current posture:** | Convicted in 1894 and executed |

---

Nothing about the room had to look criminal for the danger to work.

A kitchen table, a cup, a meal, a woman moving through the routines expected of a wife and mother. That domestic picture is what gives the Martha Needle case its force. The poison did not arrive through a stranger, a public bottle, or an exotic setting. It sat inside domestic life, where food, drink, and care could be handled without immediate suspicion. By the time the law closed around Needle in the 1890s, the case had grown beyond one death. Yet it still begins in an ordinary household, where the familiar object on the table carried more weight than any dramatic scene.

Martha Needle lived in colonial Victoria and later entered Australian crime history as one of the most notorious domestic poisoners of the era. The prosecution case and later historical accounts tied her to a pattern of deaths among husbands, children, and family members. Historical accounts and contemporary reports also tied several of those deaths to insurance payouts, and prosecutors portrayed the home as not only the place where poison could be served, but also a setting where death brought financial benefit.

That financial element matters because it gave the case a different shape from cases built mainly around jealousy, panic, or a collapsing marriage. Here, the pressure was material, at least as prosecutors and later historical accounts described it. The suspected circle around Needle's name came to include her husband, children, and members of the Lee family, even though the formal conviction was narrower than the full pattern later attached to her.

Repeated family deaths eventually stopped looking like private sorrow and started looking like a pattern. Authorities focused on arsenic, on the sequence of losses around Needle, and on the insurance benefits said to follow them. Once that happened, the case no longer read like misfortune layered over a hard life. It became a prosecution built on repetition, motive, and the belief that domestic access had been used as cover.

The decisive shift was not a single dramatic serving. It was the moment investigators began to see the kitchen as a place where profit and poisoning could meet.

**Evidence Trail**

The evidentiary center of the Needle case was the chain of deaths and the financial gain that appeared to follow them. Historical summaries, including the Public Record Office Victoria account, stress the role of insurance and the repetition of poison suspicions across multiple family members. That broader pattern gave the case its moral and public force. But the case has to stay disciplined about the legal core. As with several historic poisoner cases, not every death later associated with Needle should be treated as one giant courtroom tally.

The stronger claim is narrower. The law secured a conviction on specific poisoning charges, and the prosecution persuaded the court that arsenic had been deliberately used within the home in that count, while other deaths were discussed as part of the surrounding pattern. The broader pattern explains why the case terrified the public. The conviction is what fixed it.

## Courtroom Snapshot

Martha Needle was tried and convicted in Victoria in 1894. The prosecution case treated her as a woman who had used poison inside family life in order to collect insurance and remove dependents. The court accepted that case, and she was sentenced to death. She was later executed in Melbourne.

## Case Takeaway

In this case, the kitchen was more than a domestic backdrop. Historical accounts and prosecutors alike cast it as the place where meals, medicine, and motive could meet, with arsenic moving through ordinary household routines while insurance money shadowed the deaths. That combination is what keeps the Needle case so disturbing. The route was intimate, repeated, and profitable, turning the home from a place of care into an instrument of harm.

---

**The next case moves into modern America, where protein shakes meant to support recovery instead became part of a deeply disturbing pattern prosecutors said was leading toward murder.**

## CASE 29 CITATIONS

Public Record Office Victoria, 2024, Martha Needle -- https://prov.vic.gov.au/about-us/our-blog/martha-needle

## CASE 30

# TEN DAYS OF SHAKES

This case unsettles because it did not hinge on one dramatic moment, but on repetition, where recovery itself became shadowed by a pattern prosecutors said was steering steadily toward murder.

## PROTEIN SHAKES BUILT A MURDER CASE

### CASE DOSSIER

| | |
|---|---|
| **Case subject:** | James Craig |
| **Location:** | Aurora/Arapahoe County, Colorado, USA |
| **Key dates:** | Mar. 2023 \| July 2025 |
| **Victim(s):** | Angela Craig |
| **Method:** | Arsenic-laced protein shakes |
| **Legal status:** | Convicted |
| **Current posture:** | Convicted in 2025 and sentenced to life without parole |

The shakes were supposed to belong to health. Protein powder, water, ice, and the domestic rhythm of a couple trying to move through another ordinary week. That is what made the James Craig case so unsettling in court. Prosecutors said the route to murder was not a dramatic ambush or a public attack. It was something made in the kitchen, handed across a marriage, and repeated over days until the pattern finally became impossible to miss.

By the time Angela Craig was hospitalized, the case already had its central object. The protein shake did not just explain how the case began. It explained why the early symptoms looked confusing enough to buy time.

James Craig was a Colorado dentist. Angela Craig was his wife and the mother of their six children. In trial coverage, prosecutors described a marriage under strain, shaped by infidelity, financial pressure, and Craig's desire to leave without facing the costs of divorce.

The defense pushed back on that picture, arguing the state had built a convenient motive story around a troubled relationship and had not proved that Craig was the one who delivered the poison. That tension mattered because this was not a case driven by one confession or one witness. It was driven by how the jury interpreted a collapsing marriage, digital searches, purchases, and a sequence of medical crises that made ordinary domestic care look increasingly deliberate.

Angela Craig became gravely ill more than once in March 2023. Prosecutors said those episodes were not random medical events but escalating poisonings. AP reported that the state argued James Craig repeatedly laced her protein shakes with toxic substances, including arsenic and tetrahydrozoline, before giving her a final fatal dose of cyanide while she was hospitalized. Repetition gave the case its shape: illness, partial recovery, renewed collapse, and then a final event prosecutors said completed the pattern.

**Evidence Trail**

AP coverage describes an evidentiary spine that included toxicology showing arsenic, tetrahydrozoline, and cyanide in Angela Craig's body. Prosecutors also pointed to internet searches about poison, orders for toxic substances, jailhouse communications, and hospital surveillance images that, they said, showed James Craig carrying a syringe before Angela's condition worsened.

The defense attacked that chain at multiple points. AP reported that Craig's lawyers argued the image quality was poor, that recovered syringes did not contain poison, and that the state's witnesses were not always reliable. They also suggested Angela Craig may have taken her own life, a theory jurors ultimately rejected. What gave the case its weight was not one dramatic clue. It was the accumulation: repeated unexplained illness, poison findings, purchases, messages, and behavior that prosecutors said made sense only if the shakes were part of an intentional murder plan.

## Courtroom Snapshot

In July 2025, a Colorado jury convicted James Craig of first-degree murder in Angela Craig's death along with other charges tied to attempts to cover up the case. AP reported that prosecutors said he poisoned his wife's protein shakes over about 10 days and then delivered a final fatal dose while she was in the hospital. The defense maintained that the evidence did not directly prove Craig administered the poison and suggested the investigation had become too narrowly focused on him. The jury did not accept that position. Because first-degree murder carries a mandatory sentence in Colorado, Craig was sentenced to life in prison without the possibility of parole. The legal posture is firm: a completed conviction with a mandatory life sentence, not a still-active allegation.

## Case Takeaway

What marks this case is how poison was alleged to move through the language of self-improvement and care. A protein shake suggests routine, discipline, health, and partnership. It belongs to kitchens, gym bags, and the repeated habits couples build together. That is what gave the prosecution theory such force. The route did not need ceremony. It only needed familiarity. The jury concluded that what looked like a supportive domestic ritual had been turned into a delivery system for repeated harm. One shake might invite doubt. A sequence of illnesses, toxic findings, and a final hospital act turned that doubt into a verdict.

**From repeated attempts over days, the focus narrows to a single drink, a single moment, and a death that forced investigators to ask whether one sip had been enough.**

## CASE 30 CITATIONS

Associated Press, 2025-07-30, Colorado dentist convicted of murder after poisoning wife's protein shakes --
https://apnews.com/article/4ace26d51934756ba2e2f4a79096f03e

Associated Press, 2025-07-29, Prosecutors say financial problems and affairs led Colorado dentist to poison wife's protein shakes --
https://apnews.com/article/741e15b1cc91271164631e8223d43ffe

Associated Press, 2024-05-23, Prosecutors present evidence that Colorado dentist charged in wife's death tried to kill detective --
https://apnews.com/article/6ef88706b302e9c3b3967f58d1072bd9

## CASE 31

# JUST ONE SIP

Some cases turn on a long sequence of warning signs. This one narrowed to a single drink, a sudden death, and a question that would not go away: was this tragedy, or design?

## ONE SIP BROUGHT A MURDER TRIAL

### CASE DOSSIER

| | |
|---|---|
| **Case subject:** | Kouri Richins |
| **Location:** | Kamas / Summit County, Utah, USA |
| **Key dates:** | Mar. 2022 \| May 2023 \| Feb.-Mar. 2026 |
| **Victim(s):** | Eric Richins |
| **Method:** | Alleged fentanyl-laced cocktail |
| **Legal status:** | Charged |
| **Current posture:** | On trial in 2026 on aggravated murder and related counts; no verdict at draft date |

Prosecutors say the case turns on a drink that should have ended the evening quietly. A cocktail handed across a marriage, taken late at home, does not usually enter the record as homicide evidence.

In Summit County, prosecutors allege that is exactly what happened. They say Kouri Richins mixed a fatal dose of fentanyl into a Moscow-Mule-style drink and served it to her husband, Eric Richins, in March 2022. The case begins there because the setting is so small: one glass, one house, one married couple, and a death the state says was meant to look sudden rather than staged.

By the time the case reached trial, prosecutors had built a motive theory around money, control, and a marriage already under strain. AP reported that the state alleges Richins was heavily in debt, had taken out or expected to benefit from life-insurance policies worth close to $2 million, and wanted control over property and estate matters tied to millions more.

The prosecution also pointed to evidence that Eric Richins had changed estate planning in ways that cut against her interests. Many reports also note that, after Eric's death and before charges were filed, Kouri Richins wrote and promoted a children's book about grief, a detail that helped drive intense public attention to the case.

The defense, meanwhile, pushed back hard on the state's picture, arguing that Eric had a history of opioid use related to health problems and that the prosecution's witness chain was unreliable. That matters because this is not a conviction case. It is an active trial. All charges remain allegations, and Kouri Richins is presumed innocent unless and until proven guilty.

Eric Richins was found dead, and investigators, based on toxicology and other information, moved away from treating the death as a natural or accidental overdose and began investigating it as a possible intentional poisoning.

According to AP and Utah reporting, prosecutors say the fatal dose was delivered through a cocktail served by his wife after a dinner celebration. They also allege an earlier failed poisoning attempt involving a sandwich on Valentine's Day 2022, using it to argue a pattern of intent. It was no longer only about a husband's death. It became, in the state's telling, a case built to show both route and intent.

**Evidence Trail**
The evidentiary fight in the Richins case is one reason the file has to be handled with discipline. Prosecutors have relied on toxicology, financial records, text messages, internet searches, and witness testimony about how fentanyl was allegedly obtained. The defense has attacked the witness chain, especially claims tied to drug sourcing, and has argued the state cannot prove beyond reasonable doubt that Kouri Richins actually procured and served fentanyl.

AP reported that prosecutors used opening statements to frame the death as a financially motivated poisoning, while the defense answered that the public had heard an incomplete version of the case. That leaves the evidence trail in a live, adversarial state. The state has a prosecution theory, the defense has a rebuttal, and no jury finding had yet closed the gap between them.

## Courtroom Snapshot

As of the time of writing, reporting confirmed that a grand jury had indicted Casper-Leinenkugel on aggravated murder and numerous related charges, including attempted criminal homicide and fraud counts. AP reported that prosecutors told jurors she killed Eric Richins for money and served him a fentanyl-laced cocktail, while the defense argued that the state's central witnesses were unreliable and that Eric's own opioid history complicated the prosecution theory.

Earlier reporting showed the death penalty was not being sought. The legal posture is therefore precise and limited: charged, tried, and contested, with no verdict yet. That means every factual claim beyond the death itself and the existence of charges must stay tied to what prosecutors allege or what the defense disputes.

## Case Takeaway

One cocktail is enough to build a prosecution around motive, money, and opportunity, but not enough on its own to end the argument. Prosecutors characterize the route as simple and deliberate. The defense argues the evidentiary chain is broken. That unresolved tension defines the case. The domestic act is familiar. The legal meaning of that act was, at this stage, still being fought over in open court.

---

**The next case shifts from adult relationships to a child-centered case, where something as ordinary as apple juice in the fridge became the focus of allegations almost impossible to absorb.**

## CASE 31 CITATIONS

AP News, 2026-02-24/25, Utah murder trial opens with prosecutors alleging a fentanyl-laced cocktail killed Eric Richins --
https://apnews.com/article/55949a453ff23ac67f776058c0718fcd

AP News, 2026-02-23/24, Trial profile and defense overview in the Kouri Richins case --
https://apnews.com/article/fb8c485bf705e7bb2c57a4f038ad76a4

KSL.com timeline, jury selection and trial schedule updates --
https://www.ksl.com/article/51446543/heres-a-timeline-of-the-kouri-richins-case-as-jury-is-now-selected-for-her-murder-trial

## CASE 32

# APPLE JUICE IN THE FRIDGE

The terror here came from the fact that nothing about the setting felt unusual, until a common drink inside an ordinary home became tied to accusations almost impossible to comprehend.

## APPLE JUICE IN FRIDGE DREW CHARGES

### CASE DOSSIER

| | |
|---|---|
| **Case subject:** | Krystale El Khatib |
| **Location:** | Illinois, USA |
| **Key dates:** | Jan. 2015 |
| **Victim(s):** | Three children allegedly targeted |
| **Method:** | Alleged poisoned apple juice |
| **Legal status:** | Charged |
| **Current posture:** | Charged in 2015; verified material kept the case in allegation posture |

The juice was already in the house. That is what makes the case so unsettling.

Apple juice belongs to the everyday grammar of family kitchens, something poured without ceremony, trusted because it sits among the ordinary things children reach for every day. In Illinois in 2015, police alleged that this very familiarity made the poisoning possible. The case did not begin with an exotic substance or a stranger's delivery. It began in the refrigerator, with a common drink that police alleged had been turned into the route of harm.

At the center of the case was Krystale El Khatib, an Illinois mother accused of poisoning her children by crushing prescription pills into apple juice. The reporting in the verified source pack treated the allegations as a family-home case, not a broader public contamination scare. That distinction matters. This was not about a tainted product moving through stores or schools. It was about a private household where the person controlling the kitchen was also the person police accused of controlling the route. The pressure in the case comes from that domestic setting. Children are not meant to question the drink they are handed at home.

The children became ill, and authorities allegedly connected the symptoms to the juice. ABC News reported that police said crushed pills had been mixed into apple juice served to the children. Once that allegation entered the case, the scene in the home changed from family routine to criminal inquiry. The central object was no longer just the drink in the cup. It was the carton in the refrigerator, the means by which something familiar could have been altered before it was poured.

## Evidence Trail

Because this is a charge-stage case, the evidence has to be described narrowly and carefully. The verified reporting says police alleged that pills had been crushed and placed into the apple juice and that the children showed signs consistent with poisoning. According to the January 2015 reports, the children were treated in hospital and were expected to recover.

The case does not claim more than that because the source pack fixes the matter at the point of accusation, not adjudicated proof. What gives the case its structure is the state's allegation of route and access: the juice, the pills, the children, and the home kitchen. The strength of the case comes from that stark simplicity rather than from an overloaded backstory.

## Courtroom Snapshot

At the reporting stage captured in the verified pack, Krystale El Khatib was charged and accused of poisoning her children with crushed pills in apple juice. ABC News and 6abc both framed the matter as an active prosecution, not a resolved verdict posture. That means the case has to stop where the reliable public posture stops.

There is no conviction stated here, no jury finding, and no sentencing outcome in the locked source base. The legal posture is allegation only. The prosecution theory was that the juice was deliberately altered and served to the children. Any fuller courtroom resolution would need additional verified sourcing before it could be stated.

## Case Takeaway

What unsettles this case is not simply that juice was involved. It is that the alleged route was something already sitting in the refrigerator, part of the ordinary logic of family life before police said it became evidence. A carton, a glass, a kitchen routine, and children who had no reason to question what they were given: that combination is enough to explain why the allegation lands so hard. The charge-stage posture keeps the legal picture narrow, but the domestic route is what gives the case its weight.

---

**From a family kitchen, the story moves to a luxury hotel in Thailand, where tea service and a sealed room gave the next case the atmosphere of a locked-room mystery.**

## CASE 32 CITATIONS

ABC News, 2015-01-15, Poisoned kids: Mom crush pills in apple juice, police say -- https://abcnews.go.com/News/poisoned-kids-mom-crush-pills-apple-juice-police/story?id=28296029

6abc (WPVI), 2015-01-16, Mother accused of poisoning kids with apple juice -- https://6abc.com/post/mother-accused-of-poisoning-kids-apple-juice/477587/

## CASE 33

# TEA SERVICE IN THE HOTEL ROOM

With its sealed room, untouched details, and fatal outcome, this case carried the atmosphere of a locked-room mystery, except the deaths around the table were terribly real.

## HOTEL TEA SERVICE ENDED IN DEATH

### CASE DOSSIER

| | |
|---|---|
| Case subject: | Bangkok hotel cyanide deaths |
| Location: | Grand Hyatt Erawan, Bangkok, Thailand |
| Key dates: | July 2024 |
| Victim(s): | Six adults found dead in a hotel room |
| Method: | Cyanide in tea service or drinks |
| Legal status: | No trial |
| Current posture: | Police concluded one of the dead was the likely perpetrator in a murder-suicide; no court verdict |

The food on the table had barely been touched. That detail mattered almost immediately. In the Bangkok hotel case, the untouched dishes sat beside the real center of the case: tea service inside a closed room at the Grand Hyatt Erawan. Six people had gathered there for what appeared to be a private meeting. By the time housekeeping entered, all six were dead. The room had the look of an interrupted conversation rather than a violent struggle. That is what gives the case its force. The danger did not arrive through obvious chaos. It sat in cups waiting on the table.

The group consisted of four Vietnamese nationals and two U.S. citizens of Vietnamese origin. Thai police said the gathering was connected to a financial dispute over a failed investment project. Reporting indicated that some of the victims believed they were coming to discuss repayment and resolve the dispute outside court. That background matters because it gave the meeting a practical purpose. This was not a random hotel-room gathering and not a public attack on strangers. It was a private meeting among people who already knew one another, which made the tea service feel ordinary until it no longer could.

Cyanide traces were found in teacups and tea vessels inside the room, Reuters reported, and CCTV and staff accounts became central to the investigation. Thai authorities said one woman in the group had received the food and tea service and declined assistance preparing the tea, telling staff she would handle it herself. Soon after, the rest of the group entered. No one else was seen going in or out after that point. Once those details came together, the case narrowed around the tea service itself.

## Evidence Trail

Investigators presented an evidentiary picture that was unusually clear for a case with no surviving suspect: cyanide reported in the drinking vessels, autopsy findings of poisoning, and CCTV-based timing from the hotel. The untouched food mattered because it helped rule out the meal as the route. Staff delivered the items. One guest took control of the setup. CCTV then showed the others entering, after which none of the six emerged alive. Police also said the bodies' positions and the victims' imminent onward travel plans made a planned group suicide unlikely. The route, according to investigators, was the tea.

## Courtroom Snapshot

This is not a courtroom case in the usual sense because there was no surviving defendant to prosecute. Thai police publicly said they believed one of the six dead had poisoned the others and then died as well. Reuters reported that authorities tied the suspected motive to debt and failed investment arrangements, while also ruling out terrorism and the involvement of an outsider entering the room after the tea service. The legal posture is therefore different from a conviction case. The case rests on a police conclusion supported by forensic findings and scene evidence, not on a trial verdict. That does not make it vague. It simply means the case closes at the investigative conclusion rather than in court.

## Case Takeaway

What gives this case its force is the way poison dominated a scene inside a public-facing luxury setting. A hotel suite should feel safer than an isolated house.

A tea service should feel less threatening than an unopened bottle from nowhere. But the Bangkok case demonstrates how quickly privacy can become concealment. The room was elegant, the food was untouched, and the tea looked ready for conversation. According to investigators, that is exactly what made it work. The strongest image in the case is not the locked door. It is the cups on the table, already carrying the outcome.

---

**The next case returns to the American home, where a pitcher of margaritas and a collapsing marriage would produce another chilling allegation of poison poured in plain sight.**

## CASE 33 CITATIONS

Reuters, 2024-07-17, Thai police say cyanide killed 6 foreigners in Bangkok hotel, including suspect -- https://www.reuters.com/world/asia-pacific/thai-police-say-cyanide-killed-6-foreigners-bangkok-hotel-2024-07-17/

ABC News (AU), 2024-07-21, Six people came to Bangkok to resolve a business dispute. It ended in murder-suicide by cyanide -- https://www.abc.net.au/news/2024-07-21/six-people-came-to-bangkok-to-resolve-a-business-dispute-it-ende/104117620

The Guardian, 2024-07-17, Cyanide found in teacups shared by six found dead in Bangkok hotel -- https://www.theguardian.com/world/article/2024/jul/17/cyanide-cups-teacups-dead-bangkok-grand-hyatt-erawan-hotel-thailand

## CASE 34

# MARGARITA MURDER

Behind the image of a shared drink was a relationship under strain, and behind that strain was a prosecution case that argued poison had been folded into domestic life with deliberate calm.

## MARGARITA GLASS BECAME EVIDENCE

### CASE DOSSIER

| | |
|---|---|
| Case subject: | Cynthia Galens |
| Location: | Upstate New York, USA |
| Key dates: | 2007 \| Nov. 2010 |
| Victim(s): | David Galens |
| Method: | Antifreeze-laced margaritas |
| Legal status: | Convicted |
| Current posture: | Sentenced in 2010 to 23 years in prison |

A pitcher is the kind of object people rarely think twice about. It belonged to a late hour, a kitchen winding down, a drink mixed for home rather than display.

Margaritas in a jug suggest ease: ice beginning to melt, salt drying on the rim, two people no longer performing for anyone else. That is why the Cynthia Galens case lands as hard as it does. Prosecutors said the fatal route did not arrive through a stranger, a factory seal, or a public bottle. It sat in a shared container on a domestic counter. By the time David Galens became violently ill, the object that had signaled relaxation had already crossed into evidence.

Cynthia and David Galens were a married couple in upstate New York, and the prosecution later presented the killing as a domestic poisoning carried out inside the ordinary routines of home life. That matters because the case did not depend on spectacle. There was no crowded party, no restaurant, no public handoff, and no confusion about who had access to the drink.

The setting was small, familiar, and private. A husband could accept what was poured for him without treating the act as suspicious. That is the pressure point in the case. The relationship did not merely supply motive theory or legal context. It supplied the quiet mechanics of delivery. Sentencing coverage described the method as deliberate and intimate, and that intimacy is what gives the case its unease. A shared drink in a marriage is supposed to lower suspicion. Here, prosecutors said, it did the opposite.

Investigators ultimately focused on ethylene glycol, the toxic ingredient commonly associated with antifreeze, and that finding changed the shape of the case. Once the illness was read through that toxic route, David Galens's collapse no longer looked like a sudden unexplained medical event.

Prosecutors said antifreeze had been mixed into a jug of margaritas and served to him at home.

From that point on, the central object in the room was not simply the body or the timing of symptoms. It was the pitcher itself, and the act of mixing something into a prepared drink before it was poured.

That shift is what turns the case from domestic tragedy into a poisoning case. The danger was not hidden in an obscure laboratory process. It was hidden in a familiar vessel, already associated with sharing.

## Evidence Trail

The evidentiary case that reached the jury was not framed as rumor, atmosphere, or marital suspicion standing in for proof. Sentencing coverage treated toxicology as the spine of the prosecution's case and the margaritas as the accepted delivery vehicle. The state did not need an elaborate chain of theatrical clues to explain how the poisoning happened.

It needed the toxic findings, the drink, and the jury's acceptance that the poisoning was intentional. That distinction matters. Some poison cases remain tangled in allegation, inference, or unresolved debate. This one reached the harder ground of a courtroom result.

The evidentiary force came from the collision between chemistry and ordinariness: ethylene glycol identified as the poison, a jug of margaritas identified as the route, and a domestic setting that made the serving look unremarkable until the toxicology gave it a different meaning.

## Courtroom Snapshot

Cynthia Galens was convicted in the death of her husband and was sentenced in November 2010 to 23 years in prison. CBS News and UPI both reported the sentence after the court accepted the antifreeze-laced margarita as the central mechanism of the killing. The prosecution theory was stark in its simplicity. A wife used a shared household drink to deliver poison to her husband. Nothing in the legal posture remains open. This is not an allegation case, not a disputed historical reconstruction, and not a prosecution awaiting verdict.

The sentence fixed the case in the formal language of conviction. That finality is important because the method itself could easily have belonged to a case built out of uncertainty. A pitcher on a counter is an ordinary thing. The verdict is what forces it to remain in view as an instrument rather than an accessory.

## Case Takeaway

What makes this case memorable is not scale. It is compression. The prosecution did not need a feast, a holiday room, or a long guest list in order to describe something devastating.

It needed one vessel, one act of trust, and one toxic decision hidden inside something made for sharing. That is why the pitcher carries more weight than the garnish, the salt rim, or the familiar language of a nightcap. It held the social script of the scene. A jug of margaritas suggests that the evening has narrowed into comfort.

The court's finding put something else inside that same image: solitary intent, chemical violence, and a result that could not be recalled once the drink was swallowed. The case stands out because it shows how poisoning can stay small in appearance while becoming final in law.

---

**From tainted drinks in the United States, the story returns to Australia, where a bowl of reheated soup became central to a quieter but no less disturbing domestic case.**

## CASE 34 CITATIONS

CBS News, 2010-11-11, Woman who poisoned margarita gets 23 years -- https://www.cbsnews.com/news/woman-who-poisoned-margarita-gets-23-years/

UPI, 2010-11-11, Woman sentenced in anti-freeze killing -- https://www.upi.com/Top_News/US/2010/11/11/Women-sentenced-for-anti-freeze-killing/15471289510485/

## CASE 35

# THE REHEATED SOUP

There was nothing dramatic about the setting, only the quiet rhythm of home life. That is what makes this case so chilling, a domestic death shaped by tension, medication, and a bowl of soup later viewed very differently.

## REHEATED SOUP ENDED IN DEATH

### CASE DOSSIER

| | |
|---|---|
| **Case subject:** | Judith Ann Venn |
| **Location:** | Alexandra Hills, Queensland, Australia |
| **Key dates:** | Aug. 2020 \| Aug. 2023 |
| **Victim(s):** | Lance Venn |
| **Method:** | Soup laced with prescription medication |
| **Legal status:** | Convicted |
| **Current posture:** | Pleaded guilty to manslaughter and was sentenced in 2023 |

A pot of vegetable soup cooling in a suburban kitchen does not look like the center of a homicide case. That is what makes this one so hard to absorb.

In Alexandra Hills, the meal was familiar, homemade, and ordinary enough to belong to the background of a long marriage. Nothing in the bowl itself suggested spectacle. There was no public confrontation, no dramatic setting, no visible sign that the domestic routine had narrowed into something fatal. But by the time Lance Venn ate from the reheated soup, prosecutors would later say the decision had already been made. The serving was small. The history behind it was not. Years of strain, fear, illness, caregiving, money pressure, and exhaustion had already filled the room long before the spoon was lifted.

Judith Ann Venn and Lance Venn had been married for decades. By the time of his death in August 2020, the marriage was described in court as a place of exhaustion, fear, and worsening instability. Reporting from the sentencing hearing said Lance Venn had long lived with bipolar disorder and manic-depressive illness and that his condition had deteriorated in the previous 18 months.

The court also heard that Judith Venn had endured physical, verbal, and emotional abuse for decades while carrying the daily burden of managing the household and his care. The pressure was not a single argument or a single bad night. It was cumulative. Money was tight. Their daughters had seen the strain. He was said to wander at night, return agitated, and keep the home organized around disruption rather than calm. By the time the case reached sentencing, psychiatric evidence described Judith Venn as severely depressed, under extreme and prolonged stress, and increasingly unable to see any way out of her circumstances.

The court also heard evidence that she tended to understate the physical violence in the home. What emerges is not a sudden domestic explosion, but a household worn down over years until ordinary obligations began to feel unbearable.

The sequence that fixed the case unfolded across two mornings. On August 12, 2020, Lance Venn bought a boat from a neighbor for about $20,000, a purchase that deepened the family's financial stress. The next day, according to the facts outlined in court, Judith Venn dissolved about 50 of his prescription tablets into his favorite vegetable soup, then reheated it and served it to him. A psychologist appointment had been scheduled. Then came another night walk, another early-morning disturbance, and another message from their daughter saying he had shown up outside her house before 4 a.m. Judith replied with words to the effect of, "OK that ends it." When he returned home, she served him the soup. That is where the long domestic history narrowed into one bowl placed in front of him at the table.

## Evidence Trail

The evidence in this case was concentrated rather than sprawling. Prosecutors relied on medical evidence that Lance Venn died from an overdose delivered through the soup, using his own prescription medication. After he lost consciousness, Judith Venn slit his wrist and then attempted to take her own life; the court heard he died from the overdose caused by the soup laced with his medication rather than from the wrist wound.

Police also recovered a letter written for family members, and reporting from the sentencing hearing said she later told investigators she did not want her daughters to inherit the burden of caring for him.

The record also contained psychiatric evidence. That mattered because the case did not turn only on what she did, but on the mental state in which she did it. Experts described major depressive disorder, chronic stress, and a life shaped by prolonged abuse. The judge accepted psychiatric evidence that, by the time of the killing, she felt there was "no way out of an intolerable situation." Those details did not erase the act, but they were central to why the murder charge was downgraded and the prosecution accepted a plea to manslaughter.

**Courtroom Snapshot**
Judith Ann Venn was originally charged with murder over her husband's death at their Alexandra Hills home. In August 2023, she pleaded guilty to manslaughter in the Supreme Court in Brisbane. The prosecution case, as reported from court, was that she knowingly laced her husband's favorite vegetable soup with a fatal quantity of pills and served it to him.

The defense case centered on severe depression, prolonged abuse, and the intolerable pressure of her circumstances. Justice Frances Williams sentenced her to eight and a half years in prison and made her immediately eligible to apply for parole because she had already spent nearly three years in custody.

The legal posture gives the case a clear shape. There was no jury verdict after contest. There was a guilty plea, a sentencing record, and a court that treated the killing as unlawful while also weighing the conditions that led to it. Reporting also noted that Judith Venn, who had no prior criminal history, was 69 at sentencing and had been described as a devout member of the Christadelphian church.

## Case Takeaway

This case works by compression. The years are long. The act is short. A household can absorb fear, obligation, humiliation, untreated illness, financial strain, and daily disruption for a very long time without showing much to the outside world. Then the violence appears in a form that looks almost too ordinary to carry what it carries. A bowl of soup does that here. It holds marriage, illness, caregiving, abuse, despair, and one irreversible decision. There is no public ambush, no elaborate disguise, no theatrical staging. There is a favorite meal reheated and served across a table inside a marriage that had already been failing for years. The domestic setting does not make the act feel smaller. It makes it harder to dismiss. What remains is an unlawful killing, and the record of a life that had been closing in long before the soup was served.

---

**The next case breaks sharply from the household and expands in scale, showing how food itself could be weaponized in a deliberate public attack designed to sicken hundreds.**

## CASE 35 CITATIONS

ABC News, Judith Ann Venn jailed for killing abusive husband with soup laced with prescription medication -- https://www.abc.net.au/news/2023-08-04/judith-ann-venn-jailed-for-killing-abusive-husband-spiked-soup/102689162

ABC News, Alexandra Hills woman charged with domestic violence murder -- https://www.abc.net.au/news/2020-08-18/alexandra-hills-woman-charged-domestic-violence-murder/12568056

1News, 'Intolerable situation' led to husband's soup lacing death -- https://www.1news.co.nz/2023/08/04/intolerable-situation-led-to-husbands-soup-lacing-death/

## CASE 36

# THE SALAD BAR ATTACK

This case stands apart for its scale, showing how an everyday public food setting was turned into a weapon in a deliberate attempt to spread illness and manipulate civic life.

## SALAD BARS BECAME BIOTERROR TARGETS

### CASE DOSSIER

| | |
|---|---|
| Case subject: | 1984 Rajneeshee bioterror attack |
| Location: | The Dalles, Oregon, USA |
| Key dates: | Sept. 1984 \| 1985 \| 1986 |
| Victim(s): | 751 people sickened |
| Method: | Salmonella contamination of salad bars |
| Legal status: | Convicted |
| Current posture: | Key conspirators pleaded guilty in 1986 |

The food looked exactly as it was supposed to. Lettuce under the lights, metal trays lined up behind a sneeze guard, customers moving down the counter with the ordinary confidence of people who believe lunch is the safest part of the day.

In The Dalles, Oregon, in September 1984, that confidence became the route of attack. Diners across multiple restaurants began falling ill with severe gastrointestinal symptoms. The numbers rose too fast to feel accidental, but the setting remained stubbornly ordinary. That is what gives the Rajneeshee case its force. The delivery system was not hidden in a lab or a battlefield. It sat in salad bars, right where people expected freshness, choice, and routine.

The perpetrators were members of the Rajneeshee movement based at Rajneeshpuram, a commune in Wasco County. By 1984, tensions between the commune and local residents had hardened into political conflict. According to later federal and historical accounts, figures around Ma Anand Sheela and the commune leadership were looking for ways to weaken local opposition and influence county elections.

That background matters because the poisoning was not random cruelty and not personal domestic revenge. It was strategic contamination. The pressure in the case comes from ambition and control, from a leadership circle willing to turn public eating into a political tool. The meal route matters here not because of intimacy, but because of scale. Public trust was the target.

Health officials recognized that the outbreak was salmonella, but could not immediately explain why so many separate restaurants were involved. The Centers for Disease Control and Prevention later described how more than 750 people were sickened after salmonella was intentionally spread on salad bars in The Dalles.

That finding transformed the outbreak from a public-health mystery into a criminal case. A town-wide wave of illness stopped looking like contamination by chance and started looking like contamination by design. The salad bar itself became evidence.

## Evidence Trail

The evidentiary spine was unusually strong once the conspiracy began to break open. The CDC has described the event as a deliberate salmonella contamination campaign. The FBI later summarized it as the first and largest bioterror attack in U.S. history. Investigators tied Rajneeshee members to the spread of bacteria in restaurants and to wider testing of contamination methods.

The precision of the route is what makes the case so disturbing. The attackers did not need to poison an entire food supply chain. They only needed to touch the items people would serve themselves. That gave the case its chilling economy. The serving spoons, trays, and exposed ingredients did the rest. Once confessions and guilty pleas followed, the route was no longer a matter of inference. It was part of the admitted criminal design.

## Courtroom Snapshot

The Rajneeshee salmonella attack did not end as an unsolved outbreak. It ended with criminal accountability. In 1986, Ma Anand Sheela and Ma Puja pleaded guilty to charges related to the poisoning campaign and received prison sentences. Although 751 people were sickened, sources note that no fatalities were recorded in the Rajneeshee salmonella attack.

That detail matters because the case is not a mass-murder prosecution. It is a mass contamination case, planned and executed with political intent, then resolved through guilty pleas by key conspirators.

## Case Takeaway

The earlier cases often work through intimacy: a family table, a handed drink, a bottle meant for one person. The Rajneeshee attack keeps the same core logic of trust and ingestion, but scales it outward into a town. The delivery system is no longer a private kitchen or a relationship already under strain. It is the public promise of the salad bar itself. The mechanism never stops being ordinary food placed where people expect to eat safely. What changes is the size of the target. The logic stays the same: poison hidden inside trust, then widened into a public attack on shared routine.

From mass contamination in public, the story closes back in on a single bedside setting, where care, arsenic, and doubt would form one of Britain's most enduring poisoning controversies.

## CASE 36 CITATIONS

CDC, Investigating an Outbreak Caused by Deliberate Contamination -- https://www.cdc.gov/mmwr/preview/mmwrhtml/00000138.htm

FBI History, Salmonella Typhimurium Investigation -- https://www.fbi.gov/history/famous-cases/rajneeshee-biological-terror-attack

Oregon Encyclopedia, Rajneeshee Bioterror Attack -- https://www.oregonencyclopedia.org/articles/rajneeshee_bioterror_attack/

JAMES HAMPSTEAD

## CASE 37

# CARE, ARSENIC, AND CONTROVERSY

The tension in this case lies in the gap between appearance and accusation, where acts that looked like care were later recast as evidence in a case still argued over generations later.

## ARSENIC CASE DIVIDED PUBLIC OPINION

### CASE DOSSIER

| | |
|---|---|
| **Case subject:** | Florence Maybrick |
| **Location:** | Liverpool, England, UK |
| **Key dates:** | 1889 \| 1889 |
| **Victim(s):** | James Maybrick |
| **Method:** | Alleged arsenic poisoning |
| **Legal status:** | Convicted |
| **Current posture:** | Convicted in 1889; death sentence commuted, and the case remained deeply controversial |

The serving at the center of the Florence Maybrick case was not a party drink or a household meal.

It belonged to illness. Beef tea, beef extract, and other strengthening foods belonged to the nineteenth-century language of nursing the sick, a category of care that made them ordinary and trusted. That is what gave the case its peculiar force in 1889. If poison had been delivered there, then the route was not hidden inside celebration or appetite. It was hidden inside convalescence. From the beginning, that made the case more intimate and more difficult than a simple public murder case.

Florence Maybrick was an American-born woman married to the older Liverpool cotton broker James Maybrick. Their marriage was unhappy, and by the time James became ill, the relationship had already been marked by mistrust, infidelity, and mutual resentment.

The prosecution used that domestic breakdown to supply motive, arguing that Florence had reason to want her husband dead. But this was never a clean, closed household story. James himself had a known habit of taking arsenic, a fact that immediately complicated any attempt to separate murder from self-administered poison or existing toxic exposure. That one detail shaped the case from start to finish.

Suspicion hardened as James Maybrick's illness worsened and attention settled on what he had been given during his final days. Investigators focused on arsenic and on the foods and medicines that had passed through the sickroom. One of the most remembered details in later accounts is beef tea or beef extract associated with his care.

The prosecution pointed to foods and medicines given in the sickroom, including such preparations, as possible routes for deliberate administration. But this shift did not create clarity. It created argument. Every step forward in the state's theory seemed to open another question about access, dosing, and whether the victim's own habits had already clouded the evidence.

## Evidence Trail

The evidence trail in the Maybrick case was sufficient to secure a conviction at the time but has been judged by many later commentators as too weak or ambiguous, fueling more than a century of criticism.

Arsenic was found in James Maybrick's body, but the amount, the source, and the role it played in his death were all fiercely disputed. The prosecution said Florence had administered poison and pointed to suspicious household behavior and materials.

The defense pushed back on causation, on the significance of the arsenic levels, and on the fact that James Maybrick had taken arsenic himself. This is why the case has lasted. It sits in the uneasy space between courtroom certainty and historical doubt.

The court heard enough to convict. Later critics argued that the science and the circumstances had never quite carried the weight conviction required.

## Courtroom Snapshot

Florence Maybrick was tried in 1889 and convicted of murdering her husband. She was sentenced to death, but the sentence was quickly commuted to life imprisonment after strong public controversy and official unease about the verdict. The prosecution case succeeded in court. The conviction was real. At the same time, the case never settled into calm legal closure.

It remained one of Britain's best-known disputed poison convictions, with public campaigns and later legal historians returning again and again to the question of whether the evidence had truly proved murder beyond reasonable doubt. She was eventually released from prison after serving many years and continued to protest her innocence, which helped keep the case alive in public memory.

## Case Takeaway

What keeps the Maybrick case alive is the sickroom itself. The disputed route was tied not to a feast or a social ritual but to the foods and medicines of convalescence, where care and suspicion could occupy the same tray.

A jury heard enough to convict, yet generations of critics have argued that the science and circumstances remained too uncertain to bear the weight of conviction. That tension, between formal guilt and enduring doubt, is what gives the case its lasting power.

---

**The next case returns to Australia, where something as familiar as biscuits served at home carried a danger hidden beneath the language of comfort and routine.**

## CASE 37 CITATIONS

Historic UK, The Trial of Florence Maybrick -- https://www.historic-uk.com/HistoryUK/HistoryofEngland/The-Trial-of-Florence-Maybrick/

Encyclopaedia Britannica, Florence Maybrick -- https://www.britannica.com/biography/Florence-Maybrick

Historic trial commentary and legal-history summaries on the 1889 Liverpool

## CASE 38

# SUNDAY BISCUITS

What began in the language of domestic comfort ended in suspicion and loss, as a modest offering became tied to a case that reached far beyond the first serving.

## BISCUITS ON SUNDAY TURNED FATAL

### CASE DOSSIER

| | |
|---|---|
| **Case subject:** | Rebecca Payne |
| **Location:** | Walpeup, Victoria, Australia |
| **Key dates:** | Sept. 1, 2020 \| Mar. 2023 \| May 2023 Nov. 2024 |
| **Victim(s):** | Noel Payne |
| **Method:** | Temazepam-laced lemon biscuits |
| **Legal status:** | Convicted |
| **Current posture:** | Murder conviction stands; sentence later reduced on appeal |

The biscuits looked smaller than the case they would create. Lemon-flavored, iced, and served inside a rural household, they belonged to the ordinary language of afternoon tea.

But in Walpeup on September 1, 2020, they became the delivery system for a killing that would later be argued in detail before a Victorian jury and then revisited by the Court of Appeal. The case turns on that contrast. The object is slight. The legal record around it is not.

Rebecca Payne lived with her husband, Noel Payne, in Victoria's Mallee region. By the time the case reached trial and sentencing, the court had heard extensive evidence about a marriage marked by coercion, violence, humiliation, and control.

Reporting from both the trial and the later sentence appeal described years of abuse that shaped the defense case for mercy, even though they did not prevent the jury from finding murder. That background matters because the case is not just about poison in food. It is also about how a long pattern of domination became part of the legal explanation for what followed.

The prosecution case was that on September 1, 2020, Payne crushed temazepam into lemon biscuits and gave them to her husband. He became incapacitated. What happened next turned the death into a far larger case than a simple poisoning.

The court heard that his body was wrapped, moved, and placed in a chest freezer in the yard, where it remained for days. The shift in the case is not only the drugged serving. It is the moment concealment began.

## Evidence Trail

The evidentiary spine was accepted by a jury as sufficient to prove murder, and the Court of Appeal later declined to disturb that conviction. Prosecutors said the biscuits had been laced with temazepam and that the drugging was followed by deliberate steps to hide the body. At trial, the defense argued that Payne did not intend to kill her husband and believed he would merely sleep.

The jury rejected that position. Later sentencing coverage added more context about the household, including evidence that Noel Payne had been violently abusive and degrading over many years. On the 2024 appeal, what changed was the punishment, not the legal finding of murder: the Court of Appeal reduced her sentence but left the conviction standing.

## Courtroom Snapshot

A Supreme Court jury found Rebecca Payne guilty of murder in March 2023 after a three-week trial in Mildura. In late May 2023, Justice Rita Incerti sentenced her to 16 years in prison with a non-parole period of 10 years, while also acknowledging the severe abuse she had endured. In November 2024, Victoria's Court of Appeal reduced the sentence to 12 years with a seven-year non-parole period, finding the case was exceptional and that mercy should weigh more heavily.

The court did not overturn the conviction. By the time of resentencing, the appeal court noted that Payne had already spent more than four years in custody and would be eligible for parole in December 2027.

That is the legal posture of the case: a murder conviction still standing, with an appellate court having found that the original sentence had not fully accounted for the years of torment that shaped the offender's moral culpability.

## Case Takeaway

The biscuits carry weight. The freezer carries weight. So does the concealment, and so does the abuse record the courts accepted as real and severe. The legal outcome did not erase the killing, and the killing did not erase the conditions that preceded it. That tension is what gives the case its force. A small domestic object carried the act. The courts then had to decide how much of the life around that act belonged inside the final judgment.

---

**From one intimate act of care to another, the next case turns to an overnight infant feeding, where the private routines of home became central to allegations of profound harm.**

## CASE 38 CITATIONS

ABC News, Supreme Court jury finds Rebecca Payne guilty of murdering husband Noel Payne -- https://www.abc.net.au/news/2023-03-15/rebecca-payne-found-guilty-of-murder-in-supreme-court/102097622

ABC News, Rebecca Payne sentenced to 16 years' jail for murdering husband with drug-laced biscuits -- https://www.abc.net.au/news/2023-06-01/rebecca-payne-walpeup-murder-sentence-supreme-court/102414608

ABC News, Woman who murdered her husband with drug-laced biscuits has sentence reduced -- https://www.abc.net.au/news/2024-11-20/rebecca-payne-murder-jail-sentence-cut-temazepam-biscuits/104623072

The Guardian, Jail time slashed for Victorian woman who killed abusive husband after feeding him drug-laced biscuits -- https://www.theguardian.com/australia-news/2024/nov/20/rebecca-payne-murder-sentence-reduced-husband-freezer-death-ntwnfb

## CASE 39

# THE OVERNIGHT FEEDING

This case turns on one of the most intimate acts of care, and the shock comes from how that private routine became central to claims of profound harm.

## OVERNIGHT FEEDING LED TO MURDER CHARGE

---

### CASE DOSSIER

| | |
|---|---|
| **Case subject:** | Omayrilin Colon |
| **Location:** | Fulton County, Georgia, USA |
| **Key dates:** | Jan.-Feb. 2026 |
| **Victim(s):** | Infant son |
| **Method:** | Alleged alcohol administered during overnight feeding |
| **Legal status:** | Charged |
| **Current posture:** | Charged in 2026; case remained in allegation posture at draft date |

By the time this case entered the news, the key fact was not a household object but a toxicology reading.

In Georgia, investigators said an infant boy's blood-alcohol concentration was extremely high, a medical result that shifted the case from private tragedy to criminal allegation. From there, attention turned backward through the last feeding, the bottle, and the small overnight routine that should have ended in sleep rather than emergency response. The force of the case lies in that narrowing sequence. A night feed became the timeline investigators said mattered most.

At the center of the case is Omayrilin Colon, a Georgia mother accused in the death of her infant son. The reporting in the verified source pack places the case squarely inside the private sphere of home care. This was not a broader contamination scare, and it was not a product-liability story. The state's allegation was narrower and more intimate than that. Investigators said the person responsible for preparing the bottle was also the person responsible for altering it. That setting matters because an infant has no distance from the person who feeds him. Dependency is not just emotional context. It is part of the alleged delivery route.

The child's condition stopped looking like unexplained medical collapse and began looking, in investigators' view, like poisoning through a bottle. KOMO News reported that police alleged Colon had filled the infant's bottle with alcohol. WLOX similarly reported that authorities said the child's blood-alcohol concentration was extremely high. Once those claims entered the case, the bottle itself became the focal object. The case no longer turned on general suspicion.

It turned on what had allegedly been placed into one feeding bottle and given to a child too young to resist or question it.

## Evidence Trail

Because this is an early-stage criminal case, the evidence has to be described carefully and only in the language supported by the reporting. KOMO News and WLOX both said investigators alleged the infant was given a bottle containing alcohol and later died. Police said toxicology showed the infant's blood-alcohol concentration was extremely high, consistent with having been given a bottle containing alcohol. That is the evidentiary center as currently reported: the bottle, the toxicology, and the accusation that a caregiver prepared the route. Nothing in the source pack supports moving beyond that posture.

## Courtroom Snapshot

At the reporting stage captured in the verified pack, Omayrilin Colon had been arrested and charged in Georgia in connection with her infant son's death. KOMO and WLOX both framed the matter as an active prosecution built around the allegation that alcohol had been placed in the baby's bottle. That means the case has to stop where the reliable public posture stops. There is no conviction stated here, no jury finding, and no sentencing outcome in the locked source base. The legal posture is charged and alleged, not proved. The prosecution theory, as reported, is that the bottle was deliberately altered and served to the child. Any fuller courtroom resolution would need additional verified sourcing before it could be stated.

**Case Takeaway**

What marks this case is the overnight routine investigators said became the entire evidentiary route. The allegation does not depend on a rare poison hidden in an unusual setting. It depends on a late-night feeding, an infant unable to protect himself, and toxicology that police said pointed back to what had been prepared for him. Because the prosecution is still active, the legal posture remains narrow. But the structure of the allegation is already clear: harm was said to have moved through one of the most ordinary acts of nighttime care.

---

**And for the final case, the story returns to the American household one last time, where arsenic, family ties, and a slow pattern of decline turned domestic life into something deeply sinister.**

## CASE 39 CITATIONS

KOMO News, 2026-02-01, Mom arrested for allegedly filling infant's bottle with alcohol -- https://komonews.com/news/nation-world/mom-arrested-murder-after-allegedly-filling-2-month-old-son-bottle-with-alcohol-liquor-drink-drinking-blood-alcohol-concentration-toxic-toxicology-test-report-omayrilin-colon-atlanta-georgia-fulton-county-jail-killed-kill-fatal-trauma-investigation

WLOX, 2026-02-02, Woman accused of filling infant's bottle with alcohol -- https://www.wlox.com/2026/02/02/woman-accused-filling-3-month-olds-bottle-with-alcohol-killing-him-with-blood-alcohol-level-0179/

## CASE 40

# THE SPRINGFIELD POISONINGS

What makes this case so unnerving is how fully danger seemed embedded in home life, where the rhythms of a household began to look less like routine and more like a slow campaign of harm.

## SOFT DRINKS FED A FAMILY PLOT

## CASE DOSSIER

| | |
|---|---|
| **Case subject:** | Diane Staudte and Rachel Staudte |
| **Location:** | Springfield, Missouri, USA |
| **Key dates:** | 2012-2013 \| 2014 |
| **Victim(s):** | Mark Staudte \| Shaun Staudte \| Sarah Staudte (survived) |
| **Method:** | Arsenic-laced food and drinks |
| **Legal status:** | Convicted |
| **Current posture:** | Both entered guilty pleas and were sentenced in 2014 |

The drinks did not need ceremony to become dangerous. They belonged to the ordinary rhythm of home, the kind of glasses set down at dinner or handed across a kitchen without anyone feeling the need to look twice. In Springfield, Missouri, that familiar route became the center of a family poisoning case that ended in guilty pleas from both a mother and her daughter. The case's force comes from the way harm moved through repetition. It was not one spectacular act. It was a series of servings inside a household that should have been safest for the people living in it.

The state's case centered on Diane Staudte and her daughter Rachel. Prosecutors said they used arsenic to poison members of their own family: husband and father Mark Staudte, son and brother Shaun Staudte, and daughter and sister Sarah Staudte, who survived. By the time the case resolved, the prosecution theory had hardened into a grim domestic pattern. This was not a stranger case and not a public contamination event. It was a case built around family access, private routines, and the idea that people at the same table were not all experiencing the meal in the same way.

Illness inside the Staudte household stopped looking isolated once investigators linked repeated sickness, two deaths, and Sarah Staudte's survival into a single poisoning pattern. Mark Staudte died in April 2012. Shaun Staudte died months later in September. Sarah became violently ill but lived. Once those events were read together rather than separately, the household stopped looking unlucky and started looking structured.

That shift mattered because the route was not a single dramatic meal or one obvious delivery left at a door. Prosecutors said arsenic had been introduced over time through drinks and other family consumables inside the home. The delay between attacks helped blur the pattern at first.

What finally brought the case into focus was repetition: the same household, the same shrinking circle of victims, and the same ordinary domestic setting appearing again and again in the background.

## Evidence Trail

The evidentiary spine was strong enough to end the case without trial. Reporting on the pleas said prosecutors tied the poisonings to arsenic administered through drinks and other consumables in the home, with the pattern becoming visible only after investigators stepped back and treated the illnesses as connected rather than separate tragedies.

Concern from people outside the household about the unusual cluster of illnesses helped prompt the deeper investigation that ultimately exposed the poisoning pattern.

Once law enforcement began investigating, the case widened from family misfortune into a deliberate poisoning prosecution. Sarah Staudte's survival was critical. A surviving victim turned the household chronology into something investigators could test against medical evidence, timelines, and statements.

The co-conspiracy also gives the case a distinct shape. This was not a lone poisoner moving silently through a kitchen. It was a mother and daughter, according to prosecutors and then by their own guilty pleas, acting inside the same domestic space. That relationship changes the temperature of the case. It turns repetition into something coordinated, not merely secretive, and helps explain why the pattern held long enough to kill twice before the house itself became the subject of suspicion.

**Courtroom Snapshot**

In 2014, Diane Staudte pleaded guilty to first-degree murder for the death of Mark Staudte, second-degree murder for the death of Shaun Staudte, and assault for poisoning Sarah Staudte. Rachel Staudte also pleaded guilty to related charges for her role in the poisonings. Major reporting said the two admitted that arsenic had been used within the family home and that the poisonings unfolded across months. Diane Staudte received multiple life terms, while Rachel Staudte received separate prison sentences. The legal posture is settled: a guilty-plea case with a fixed outcome, not an allegation and not a mystery left open for later reinterpretation.

**Case Takeaway**

What makes the Staudte case so grim is how repetition became its own form of concealment. One drink may not reveal the pattern. One death may not reveal it either. But once the illnesses line up and the household is read as a system rather than a sequence of bad breaks, the ordinary domestic route becomes unmistakable.

The drinks belonged to family routine, which is what let the pattern hide for so long. Nothing had to look staged or ceremonial. The poison could move through the most familiar gestures in the house, and that is what makes the case feel so cold once the verdict is in.

---

## CASE 40 CITATIONS

ABC News, 2014, Missouri mom and daughter plead guilty in arsenic poisoning deaths -- https://abcnews.go.com/US/missouri-mom-daughter-plead-guilty-arsenic-poisoning-deaths/story?id=23162546

CBS News, 2014, Diane Staudte and daughter plead guilty in family poisonings -- https://www.cbsnews.com/news/diane-staudte-rachel-staudte-plead-guilty-in-fatal-family-arsenic-poisonings/

# EPILOGUE

The crimes in this book do not linger because food and drink were involved. They linger because food and drink were trusted.

That is what gives these cases their peculiar weight. Meals, drinks, desserts, bottles, and cups are not neutral objects in daily life. They carry ritual with them. They belong to care, family, hospitality, recovery, celebration, and routine. They pass through homes, workplaces, cafés, hospitals, hotel rooms, and public spaces with an assumption so basic it rarely needs to be spoken aloud: this is safe.

In these forty cases, that assumption failed.

Sometimes it failed inside marriage. Sometimes inside family. Sometimes in friendship, at work, or in public life. Sometimes the method was quiet and patient. Sometimes it was swift. Sometimes one serving changed everything. Sometimes the meaning of what happened only came into focus later, when symptoms, toxicology, witness accounts, or simple repetition made the pattern impossible to ignore.

What makes these crimes so hard to forget is not only the harm they caused, but the transformation of the object at the center. The cheesecake, the curry, the cocoa, the Christmas cake, the milkshake, the teapot, the salad bar. Once those objects entered the record, they stopped belonging only to ordinary life.

They became evidence. They became symbols. They became the point where trust and violence met.

That shift is part of what true crime returns to again and again. Not only what was done, but how it was made possible. Not only who died, but how the setting itself was used. These cases remind us that some of the most unsettling crimes are not those that arrive with the greatest spectacle, but those that move through the most familiar channels.

A person can guard against obvious threat.

It is far harder to guard against what looks like kindness, habit, or care.

That is why so many of the stories in this book feel intimate, even when the cases are well known. Their power comes from proximity. The objects involved are small enough to recognize instantly. Most people have poured them, served them, accepted them, or placed them in front of someone else. They belong to the shared grammar of daily life. When that grammar is corrupted, the crime seems to travel further than the room where it happened.

These stories also reveal something essential about poisoning and contamination cases. They are often less about force than about access. They depend on closeness, timing, patience, and the victim's lack of alarm. That can make them seem almost quiet at first glance. They are not quiet at all. Their violence often lies in the calm required to carry them out.

To alter food. To lace a drink. To use nourishment, comfort, or routine as cover for harm. That is betrayal with an unmistakable signature.

And yet the purpose of this book has never been to leave the reader suspicious of every shared table or offered cup. It is to document, examine, and understand a distinct category of crime, one in which ordinary rituals became the route through which fear entered. Some of these cases are remembered because of scale. Others because of cruelty. Others because they remain debated, disputed, or difficult to close completely. Together they reveal how thin the line can be between the familiar and the unthinkable when trust is deliberately exploited.

That is the thread running through all forty casefiles.

Not only poison. Not only murder. Trust, misused.

The table has always been one of the oldest symbols of human closeness. It is where people gather, celebrate, negotiate, reconcile, keep routines, lower their guard, and assume for a moment that they are safe enough to eat and drink without fear. That is why the crimes in this book feel so invasive. They did not merely enter daily life. They used daily life as cover.

Long after the verdict, the appeal, the headline, or the historical argument, that is often what remains.

A cup on a saucer. A plate set down. A bottle in the refrigerator. A glass raised in celebration. A lunch packed as usual. An object so ordinary it should never have had to bear the weight of a criminal case.

And yet here they are.

Forty reminders that some of the darkest crime scenes do not begin with forced entry, obvious menace, or visible struggle.

Sometimes they begin when something is served.

# IF YOU NEED SUPPORT

Some of the cases in this book involve domestic violence, coercive control, and abuse within intimate or family relationships.

If you or someone you know is affected by domestic or family violence, help may be available in your country through a crisis line, domestic violence service, or emergency support provider.

IMPORTANT: If you are in immediate danger, contact your local emergency services.

To find a verified helpline in your country, visit the **Find A Helpline** website, choose your country, and select the **"Abuse & domestic violence"** topic.

# ACKNOWLEDGMENTS

This book was built from long hours of reading, cross-checking, drafting, and revising across cases that span decades, countries, and very different legal and historical records.

My thanks go to the journalists, court reporters, historians, archivists, and researchers whose work helped preserve these stories in the public record. True-crime writing depends on that record, and on the people who do the slow work of assembling it clearly.

Thanks also to the early readers and behind-the-scenes support who helped shape this project into a stronger and more disciplined book.

And finally, thank you to the readers who continue to make room for serious true crime and narrative nonfiction that treat disturbing material with care, structure, and respect.

# ABOUT THE AUTHOR

James Hampstead writes casefile-driven narrative nonfiction focused on true crime, criminal history, and the darker edge of ordinary life.

His work is especially drawn to cases in which trust, intimacy, routine, or belief are manipulated for criminal ends, and to the ways familiar settings can become the backdrop for extraordinary harm. Rather than chase sensation for its own sake, he is interested in how real crimes take shape, how they are remembered, and why some continue to echo long after the verdict, the headline, or the public attention has faded.

*Crimes Where Food and Drink Masked Murder* is part of a broader nonfiction approach under the James Hampstead name, exploring crimes shaped by betrayal, access, concealment, and the corruption of the familiar.

# IF YOU FOUND THESE CASEFILES COMPELLING

Thank you for reading *Crimes Where Food and Drink Masked Murder.*

If you found these casefiles engaging, thoughtful, or difficult to put down, please consider leaving an honest review where you purchased the book. Even a short review helps more readers discover this book.

Thank you for your support.

9 781764 573962